The Services Economy: Lever to Growth

The Services Economy: Lever to Growth

(translated from the French "*Les services, nouvelle donne de l'économie*," by the author)

Jacques Nusbaumer

Kluwer Academic Publishers
Boston   Dordrecht   Lancaster

Distributors

for the United States and Canada: Kluwer Academic Publishers, 101 Philip Drive, Assinippi Park, Norwell, MA 02061

for the UK and Ireland: Kluwer Academic Publishers, MTP Press Limited, Falcon House, Queen Square, Lancaster LA1 IRN, UK

for all other countries: Kluwer Academic Publishers Group, Distribution Centre, P.O. Box 322, 3300 AH Dordrecht, The Netherlands

The views expressed in this book are those of the author and do not in any way commit the organization that employs him.

Library of Congress Cataloging in Publication Data

Library of Congress Cataloging-in Publication Data

Nusbaumer, Jacques, économiste.
  The services economy.

  Translation of: Services, nouvelle donne de l'économie.
  Bibliography: p.
  Includes index.
  1. Service industries.   I. Title.
HD9980. 5. N8713 1987   338.4'6   86-21397
ISBN 0-89838-192-4

Martinus Nijhoff Publishing, 101 Philip Drive, Assinippi Park, Norwell, MA 02061

PRINTED IN THE UNITED STATES.

To Tamara

Contents

Tables and Figures

The Services Economy: Lever to Growth

1 SERVICES: LEVER TO GROWTH

The changeover from one type of economy to another is seldom perceptible at the time it occurs. In advanced societies, services activities represent up to two-thirds of national product (figure 1–1). They have supplanted industry in the role of engine of growth. But this phenomenon has almost gone unnoticed by economists or governments up to now, and it remains largely unexplained. In classical economic theory, services were considered to be unproductive.[1] This point of view influenced the methods of analysis of production as well as statistical research, so that very few researchers were interested in the activities of services as sources of value, and the data available on these activities remained scant and fragmentary.[2] The concepts devised to explain the production of goods cannot necessarily be applied to the nonmaterial production of services. Two questions arise which this book tries to answer: what is it that constitutes the essential element of a service as a product and how can one assess the value of the latter?

The systematic exploitation of intelligence and knowledge is the main cause of the importance that services have acquired in the production of advanced economies. Science and technology are dynamic supply factors, while education and training have a similar impact on demand. Any human

1

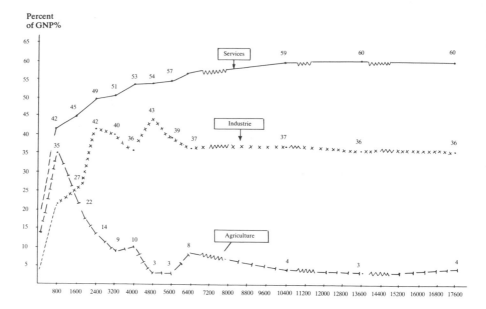

GNP per capita (averages for lower intervals)

Note: The sums of the averages do not always total 100 due to the incompleteness of data.

Sources: World Bank, *World Development Report, Washington, D.C., 1983.* Not including data for high income oil exporters and for Eastern countries.

Figure 1–1. Distribution of Gross National Product (GNP) by Main Sectors of Activity According to Level of GNP per Capita in U.S. Dollars, 1981

activity constitutes a service in the sense that it produces a tangible or intangible result, marketable or nonmarketable, but the services provided by the work of the unskilled laborer cannot be put on the same level as those of an engineer or a lawyer. Their content in human capital differs, and their degree of homogeneity is inversely proportional to that content. In addition, work experience, of which industrial discipline is an essential aspect in modern economies, provides the basis for more detailed differentiations within each category of activity. In new economies where services are predominant, primary labor can no longer be used as a standard of value as in the industrial economy analyzed by Marx. The new unit of work remains badly defined, but clearly it is more closely related to knowledge than to an individual worker's physical skill. With hindsight, this appears always to have been the case, but the obsession with material production has long concealed the true origin of value added.

For two centuries, economic theory has reflected (always with a certain delay) the evolution of conditions of production in dominant economies. From Quesnay to Marshall, via Ricardo and Marx, it sought to identify the elements that constitute the basis of value in an economic and political context characterized by the systematic dismantling of the economic and social structures of the *Ancien Régime*. Today, while the transition toward a services society is nearing completion in many countries, the concepts that should serve as frames of reference for future policymaking by governments remain to be worked out.

It is true that the role of knowledge in production has been recognized for a long time.[3] Alfred Marshall already alluded to it. It is already 30 years since the theory of human capital was developed under the leadership of Gary Becker.[4] More recently, discussions on the Leontief paradox[5] brought to light the importance of the qualitative aspect of the labor factor, too long considered as simple supplier of a more or less homogeneous "work force." Finally, the Minhas[6] theory of factor-intensity reversals in manufacturing also can be traced back to the increase in the share of human capital compared with physical capital and unskilled labor, although this relationship remains implicit in his statement. At the macroeconomic level, the importance of the residual factor in economic growth has also been recognized for a long time. But generally speaking, research and reflections on this subject have remained without effect on the economic development policies of governments, either in the industrialized countries or in the Third World. Apart from Theodore Schultz, there are few economists who have recommended an active policy of improvement of the quality of man based on these theories.

There are two ways of considering the role of services in economic development. On one hand, they can be regarded as complementary to the production of goods, either as independent activities or as activities integrated into the process of production of goods, whose output is directly incorporated in the value of the goods. On the other hand, services can be seen as autonomous activities undertaken in response to a specific demand, which may or may not be complementary to the demand for goods.

According to certain estimates, at least 50 percent of the final value of the manufactured products exported by advanced countries are made up of services (table 1–1).

The increase in the share of wages in national income reflects, at least partly, the increase in the income of skilled labor (table 1–2).

Table 1–1.   Share of Human Capital in Total Capital Employed in the Manufacture
of Goods Exported by 36 Representative Countries[1]

Category of Goods	Human Capital/ Total Capital	Share in Total Exports of the 36 Countries (Percentage)
1. Paper and articles of paper	0.411	4.3
2. Chemicals and their derivatives	0.444	11.8
3. Petroleum, coal, and their derivatives	0.447	2.4
4. Articles of stone and of glass	0.458	1.4
5. Metals	0.478	10.0
6. Wood and articles of wood	0.520	3.2
7. Articles of rubber and of plastics	0.646	2.4
8. Textiles	0.655	7.5
9. Transport equipment	0.700	19.0
10. Nonelectrical machinery	0.743	14.8
11. Articles of metal	0.747	1.7
12. Leather and articles of leather	0.747	0.8
13. Miscellaneous manufactures	0.758	2.5
14. Instruments and apparatus	0.787	2.8
15. Printing and publishing	0.811	1.4
16. Electrical equipment and machinery	0.812	9.7
17. Furniture	0.828	1.0
18. Apparel	0.855	2.3
Average for all categories	0.658	100.0[2]

1. Eighteen developed countries and 18 advanced developing countries, classified as follows: developed—Australia, Austria, Belgium, Canada, Denmark, Finland, France, Germany (Fed. Rep. of), Ireland, Italy, Japan, Netherlands, Norway, Portugal, Sweden, Switzerland, United Kingdom, United States of America; developing—Argentina, Brazil, Colombia, Greece, Hong Kong, India, Israel, Korea, Malaysia, Mexico, Morocco, Pakistan, Philippines, Singapore, Spain, Taiwan, Turkey, Yugoslavia.

2. Sums may not add to 100 due to rounding.

Source: Balassa, B. *A "Stages Approach to Comparative Advantage.* World Bank Staff Working Paper No. 256. Washington, D.C., May 1977.

Although this is a gradual phenomenon, it relates to a qualitative change in human nature, whereby what may be called for short "cerebral force" becomes more important than physical force as a factor of production. Such a change is important, of course, not only from the point of view of analyzing the motive forces behind economic production and growth as generators of welfare but also from the point of view of defining appropriate economic policies to encourage the development of new productive capacities. For it is

Table 1-2. Share of Labor Income in GNP,[1] 1960-80 (Percentages)

(1) Per Capita Income (in 1982 U.S. Dollars) and Selected Countries	(2) Share of Labor Income in GNP (Percentages)	
	(a) in 1960	(b) in 1980
260 (India)	75	68[2]
860 (Morocco)	32[3]	33
1,180 (Jamaica)	49	52
1,700 (Rep. of Korea)	32	37
2,250 (Mexico)	31	36
4,420 (Greece)	29	38
5,640 (Spain)	45	55
7,700 (New Zealand)	49	56
9,110 (United Kingdom)	60	61
11,400 (Canada)	52	55
12,820 (United States)	59	62
14,870 (Sweden)	54	64
17,430 (Switzerland)	52	61

1. The figures in column 2 are taken as an indication of the average income per employee, which is itself related to the average level of skill.

2. 1979.

3. 1970.

Sources: IBRD. *World Development Report, 1982*. Washington, D.C., 1983; and United Nations. *Yearbook of National Accounts Statistics, 1980*, vols. I and II. New York, 1983.

obvious that the processes of creation of value controlled by intelligence do not obey the same rules as the processes based on the use of physical, human, or mechanical force.

This applies to the processes of accumulation of capital as well as to the nature of the services produced by individual economic agents. Also affected are the relationships between owners and managers of physical capital and owners and managers of human capital, it being understood that the latter comprise researchers, teachers, scientific personnel, managers, controllers, and at least part of the operatives.[7]

With the development of nonmaterial productive resources in the form of practical knowledge and analytical ability of man, new needs begin to emerge. At the production stage, complementary relationships between the knowledge of the agent and the physical capital he uses are reinforced as machines becomes more complex and more subtle to handle. A standard example is that of the computer. Because it is a simple tool at the beginning,

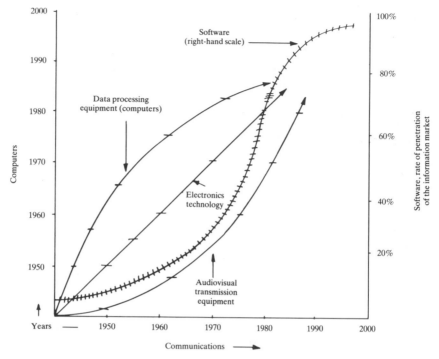

Source: Chr. de Jong, Step J.–M. [1983, pp. 68–69].

Figure 1–2. Trends in Data Processing Technology and in Communications and Software Technology and Projections to the Year 2000

a good employee with adequate technical training and an elementary mathematical education (analyst-programmer) could make it function. But in their most modern and sophisticated versions, computers with great storage and calculation capacity require software which only operators with advanced scientific training can master (figure 1–2). Thus, as the tool increases in complexity, demand for highly qualified personnel (software engineers) also increases. Moreover, as the use of various types of computers, i.e., from the simplest to the most complex, becomes widespread, the general level of skill required of personnel in the data processing sector rises, the quality of the average worker evolving with the tool.

The development of knowledge also involves an increase in the demand for consumer services. This is generally ascribed to the rise of income per capita, which would allow the average consumer to dispose of a sufficient

Table 1–3. Share of Services in Household Consumption, 1960–80

Countries	GNP/Per Capita U.S. Dollars 1982	Services in Percent of Total Final Consumption 1960	1980
India	260	15,7	16,5
Thailand	770	18,9[2]	18,6
Korea (Rep. of)	1,700	22,6	27,5
Greece	4,420	29,6	32,0
Italy	6,960	n.d.	30,9[1]
United Kingdom	9,110	32,7	39,7
Japan	10,080	42,4[3]	49,2
United States	12,820	40,4	47,1
Norway	14,060	29,2[3]	32,7
Sweden	14,870	31,3[4]	34,2

1. 1976.
2. 1975.
3. 1970.
4. 1965.

Source: UNO. Yearbook of National Accounts Statistics, 1980, vol. II. New York, 1983.

amount of income to satisfy, over and above his material needs, nonmaterial needs related to his enjoyment of leisure, or "time off" as it is often referred to nowadays (table 1–3). This explanation, which is based on the well-known correlation between per capita income and the share of services in household consumption, is not entirely satisfactory. New microcomputer owners are equally attracted by the tool as an object as they are by the possibilities it offers to better understand and manage their time or their assets; correspondingly, a demand for software is based less on the privilege of money than on that of intelligence.

The social changes that result from this evolution of demand are not immediately perceptible. At the level of employment, it is obvious that unsuited personnel are condemned to either improve their training or move down both professional and wage scales.[8] This being said, it is not certain that personnel trained to new techniques will find more outlets in independent service firms than in goods producing firms. This depends on the extent to which the application of the new knowledge is integrated into the operations of these firms or, on the contrary, is carried out by independent service firms. The factors that influence the creation of independent service firms remain obscure. The possibility of making economies of scale in the production of specific services is not a sufficient explanation if one takes into account the fact that the more sophisticated the services are, the more they are adapted to the specific needs of the consumer or individual user, which excludes the possibility of mass production.

Generally speaking, division of labor is a datum which is still insufficiently explained. The economic role of organization, know-how, and specialization pertains to the quality of the services performed by production agents. The content in experience and knowledge of these services can be a useful indicator of factor productivity, but it does not suffice to explain why the supply of certain services remains closely connected to the production of goods while others are increasingly supplied autonomously.

Everything cannot be explained by economics, and the demand for services is also political. The right to education and to health is not invoked for the sole purpose of producing more but also of making better use of the right to live. The borderline between welfare and productivity is not clear-cut when the protection and the improvement of the individual are at stake. This is why many service activities whose economic output is difficult to evaluate using the criteria applied to the production of goods, such as the criterion of opportunity cost, have recognized positive effects on growth in the form of external economies.

Much research will still be necessary before the nature of service activities is fully elucidated and reliable methods of measurement of their contribution to economic and social welfare are developed. The approach followed in this book is therefore exploratory rather than didactic. Certain concepts are advanced which are derived from observation of the workings of modern economies and from a necessarily superficial analysis of the scant statistical data available. To improve knowledge of services, it is necessary to have a better understanding not only of their real place as a distinct sector in human activity but also to promote an exchange of ideas on the principles that govern their development. If it does nothing more than stimulate thinking on these problems, this book will have fulfilled its purpose.

Notes

1. See Adam Smith (1960), in particular chapter III of book II. Marx (1952) takes the same view when he relegates into the "superstructure" all activities which are remote, albeit slightly, from material production. Samir Amin at least partly embraces this viewpoint in *Le développement inégal*, p. 173 and 212–214.

2. Consequently, governments have always shown little eagerness to promote and develop service activities. On this point, see Margaret Hall (39).

3. See Theodore W. Schultz, *Investing in People, The Economics of population* (Berkeley: University of California Press, 1981), and other works quoted therein.

4, 5, 6. See Becker (1962), Minhas (1963), and also Abramowitz (1957), Kuznets (1960), and Denison (1970) in the Bibliography. Leontief's argument is presented for the first time in "Factor proportions and the structure of American trade," a study published in 1956 and reproduced in *Input-Ouput Economics* (New York: Oxford University Press, 1966).

7. Not to speak of the fact that the simplest kind of work, that of the unskilled laborer, also benefits from a certain capital of experience as well as from the capital of knowledge embodied in the simple machines that he/she uses.

8. On this point, see *"Les cancres du progrès,"* *Le Monde*: 19 June 1983, iv.

2 SERVICES: WHAT ARE THEY?

Common Characteristics of Services

Analysts recognize that, as of now, there is no precise definition of the notion of service activity to speak of, nor any appropriate indicators of the unit value of various services. The valuation of services output is therefore very imprecise, and the conclusions drawn from existing data are necessarily tentative. In order to identify the source of the problems, let us look at them one by one.

Market, Nonmarket, and "Free" Services

The current lack of understanding of services is not due alone to the little attention devoted up to now to service activities by economists and statisticians. The nature of services is such that traditional methods of calculation based on the counting of physical quantities are inapplicable. Whereas the quantity of physical material incorporated in goods or the number of goods produced can be calculated exactly because services are intangible, their "quantity" can only be measured in terms of the duration and intensity of

11

the service functions supplied to the user. In addition, while it is possible to circumscribe the duration and intensity of service functions performed for the purpose of defining a unit of service, the limits so fixed are often arbitrary because the more or less complete character of a particular service act is largely a question of subjective interpretation on the part of the user.

On the other hand, the notion of intrinsic value, which is applicable to a good and which can be defined as the market value of which the good is the physical support, does not apply to a service which does not have an independent existence beyond the individual service act which alone determines its content. If it is true that one can establish a parallel between the value of a good and the value of a service on the basis of the notion of utility, there are also in this respect very great differences between a good and a service. The utility of a good depends on the physical and mechanical qualities incorporated in that good which in turn determine the usefulness of the good for the user. By contrast, the utility of a service only depends on the way it is being provided or supplied. Moreover, the qualities of a good are durable since they depend on the physical characteristics of the good, whereas the qualities of a service are as transient as the service itself. Consequently, it is difficult to compare the value of two services as can be done for two objects or goods serving the same purpose, and, in the absence of a precise definition of the quantity and objective value of services, it is not easy to evaluate their share of national output.

It must be emphasized, however, that the problem is not quite the same depending on the role that services play in the production process. The value of many services which are supplied within goods producing enterprises is incorporated in the value of the goods produced by these enterprises at the cost of the primary factors used to supply them. These factors add value to the goods produced exactly as the workers and machines used on the shop floor do. A priori, therefore, there is no doubt as to the unit cost of services supplied by the office and managing staff of a firm, although these may not be calculated separately.[1]

Things are different in the case of services supplied by specialized service firms (banks, insurance companies, shippers, etc.). In view of the nonmaterial character of their output, it is not possible a priori to calculate the unit cost of the factors used by these enterprises. One can, of course, calculate the salaries paid and the depreciation of the physical goods used, as well as eventually the price paid for intermediate services supplied by other specialized firms of the sector. But the distinction between cost of factors and the objective value of services supplied by these factors is difficult to establish in view of the fact that the notion of unit of service is imprecise.

This being said, from an economic point of view, the very existence of

Table 2–1. Functional Classification of Services[1]

	Primary Services	Intermediate Services	Final Services
Internationally tradable services	Repairs (12)	Transport (1) Insurance (4) Financial services (5) Business services (6) Data processing (7) Rental services (8)	Transport (1) Insurance (4) Financial services (5) Rental services (8) Recreation services (13)
Services performed on site	Construction (9)	Auxiliary services (2) Dispatching services (3) Real estate (10) Wholesale and retail trade (11) Administration (15)	Real estate (10) Wholesale and retail trade (11) Recreation services (13) Domestic and personal services (14) Administration (15)
Durable services		Insurance (4) Financial services (5) Data banks (7) Rental services (8) Real estate (10) Administration (15)	Insurance (4) Financial services (5) Rental services (8) Real estate (10) Administration (15)
Nondurable services	Construction (9) Repairs (12)	Transport (1) Auxiliary services (2) Dispatching services (3) Business services (6) Wholesale and retail trade (11) Data processing (7)	Transport (1) Wholesale and retail trade (11) Recreation services (13) Domestic and personal services (14)

1. The abbreviated descriptions of different service categories are followed by a number corresponding to the items listed on pages 18–19. The repetition of a category in different boxes of the table indicates that *some* of the services in that category meet the corresponding classification criterion.

firms specialized in the supply of services is justified by the fact that these firms can supply services to the users at lower cost for a comparable utility or of a superior utility for an equivalent cost. Logically, one must assume that for a given price the unit cost of services supplied by specialized firms is lower than the services supplied within goods producing firms or, amounting to the same thing, that for a given cost the specialized firms are able to supply a greater quantity of services of the same type than goods producing firms. If this is so, any estimation of the real value of output of services based on the sole cost of factors used by the specialized enterprises involves a downward bias which must be corrected to take into account the greater "quantity" of services supplied by the factors they employ, in other words, the greater productivity of these factors. It is not a question of artificially inflating the turnover of service enterprises, which is a datum, but rather of identifying the economic gains or benefits resulting from the division of labor between service enterprises and goods producing enterprises through relevant indicators of the volume of output in terms of units of services. Table 3–1 points to ways of solving this problem.

Apart from the analysis of service activities on the basis of the classical tenets of production theory, it is appropriate to consider to what extent the concepts applied to the marketing and international trade of goods are relevant to the marketing and trade of services. In particular, it is important to examine how the global competitiveness of economies which have witnessed a marked development of service activities may have been modified compared to other economies with more traditional production and consumption structures.

This raises the question of the place of services in the long-term development process as it has been observed to this day, or as it can be reconstituted from the comparative analysis of countries at different levels of development. One striking fact is the very important place that certain services occupy in the total production of less-developed economies.

Beyond a certain stage, there is evidence of a process of *internalization* of many services into producing firms and into the homes of consumers before one sees a very diversified service sector reappear in more advanced economies. Clearly, not always the same services appear at the beginning and end of the process, nor is their real contribution to global welfare at different stages of development the same. What remains to be explained is the nature and the quantitative importance of this contribution, so that one can understand why certain services appear to be, once and for all, internalized from a certain stage of development onward, whereas others are the subject of a new division of labor in more advanced economies.

Technological progress, particularly progress in the technologies which are integrated in the "work force" of factors of production (human capital), is certainly largely responsible for this phenomenon. However, the exact relationship between technology and the division of labor between the goods and the services sectors remains ill-defined. It is probably prudent to avoid a certain Rostowian determinism in the consideration of these problems.

While it is not easy to provide precise answers to the many questions that can be raised about the role of marketable services in the economy, it is even less easy to define the role of nonmarket services or "public" services whose principal characteristic is that the range of their use is indeterminate. For example, one never exactly knows the number and identity of the listeners of a radio program, nor the real effect on the security of property and individuals of an increase by, say, 100 men in the municipal police force. The evaluation of the "production" of the services in question is not fundamentally different from that of other services, but two important indicators of the scale of production, i.e., the number and the quality of the consumers, are lacking. Given the fairly widespread tendency toward increased intervention by governments in the economy, it is important to be able to measure the real contribution of governments to total output. Indeed, common sense will not admit that the gross domestic product of a country should be automatically reduced by the mere fact that a certain number of activities formerly carried out for profit have fallen into the public domain. It will therefore be necessary to examine in what way the so-called public services can be take into account in the framework used to analyze the role of marketable services in market economies.

Finally, it will be necessary to take into account certain analyses of service activities such as those found in recent research by the Club of Rome. Particularly relevant in this respect are the attempts to revise the notion of welfare in terms of the global evolution of the common heritage of mankind or D + P (Dowry and Patrimony) described by Orio Giarini [1980] in his book *Dialogue on Wealth and Welfare*. Their aim is to include nonmonetary activities of the private sector in the calculation of global welfare, covering a great number of services of a more or less transient character depending on the social class concerned (household work, do-it-yourself, etc.). It also integrates the "invisible" economy, essentially composed of services, into the monetized sector, by defining it as a form of subsidy to the legal economy [Giarini, 1980, p. 237], as opposed to nonmonetized activities which are outside it.

This classification brings out the notion of the "usage value" of production which measures net wealth and welfare in Orio Giarini's system. The theoretical interest of the demonstration is that it underlines the productive character of service activities—including "services" supplied free by nature (water, air, etc.) which it equates with that of goods producing activities—and introduces the concept of "stocks of services" (natural resources) [Giarini, 1980, p. 155].

In certain respects, the reasoning followed in this book is similar, since the search for a materialized expression of the output of services as a source of net accretion to total output leads to the rehabilitation of services as basic elements of material well-being, in contrast to the notion of unproductive activities to which Adam Smith wanted to confine them.

Primary, Intermediate, Final, Durable, and Nondurable Services

Leaving the field of general analysis, we can distinguish several types of services which easily fit the main economic categories currently utilized to classify goods. At the production level there are primary services, intermediate services, and final services. At the consumption level a distinction can be made between durable or continuous services and services destined to an immediate and finite utilization.

Primary services are nothing more than work supplied by factors of production in every sector of economic activity, including machines (physical capital) and land.[2] These services are common to the production of goods and "services" in the sense of a sector of activity as we understand it here. Intermediate services are activities that constitute an indispensable complement to the production of goods or other services, such as storage, financing, transport, telecommunications, maintenance, and cleaning. A great number of services enter into this category, in particular all the services linked to the marketing and distribution of goods, but also accounting services, legal services, and research services whose role grows proportionately to the complexity of modern economic relationships. Final services are those that play no direct role in the output of goods and services but which are basic elements in the welfare and quality of life of the final consumer. They include marketable services, such as entertainment and tourist services, as well as nonmarketable services, such as municipal police and the fire brigade.

Finally, whereas the majority of services have a short usage period and are not transferable like goods, there are certain services (market or nonmarket) whose effects are more durable, such as insurance, financial guarantees, legal protection, data banks, or public order, national defense, etc., and which play a role in both the production and the final consumption of other goods or services. These represent the more capital-intensive part of the sector of services, and their development has generally followed a course parallel to that of the most dynamic branches of the other major sectors of economic activity.

It is clear that the previous classification is not rigorous and that certain services can appear simultaneously in several categories. There are as yet no agreed conventions in this regard. In fact, analysts do not always agree among themselves on the very notion of service; for example, certain analysts exclude transport or banking services from the coverage of this notion. For our part, we will use a wide definition that covers all activities not *directly* related to the production of goods, that is, all services other than those supplied by labor and machines used in the manufacture and processing of raw materials and those imputed to national resources employed in these productive operations, such as land for agriculture, water for the production of electricity, etc.[3]

Generally speaking, it is clear that services which contribute to the production of goods or to the production of other services are elements of global supply, whereas those not linked to any particular process of production, such as entertainment services or sports, are components of final demand. In both cases, there exist relationships of complementarity and substitution either between various services or between certain services and certain goods. However, these relationships evolve in accordance with the development of technology and the influence of other factors. For instance, intermediate services complementary to goods and incorporated in the value of such goods at the handicraft production stage, such as design, research, and product-testing services, may be dissociated from them at a later stage of technological development and may substitute for them in the form of R & D (research and development), engineering services, technical consulting services, laboratory testing services, etc. The separate sale of these services partly displaces the sale of goods to the final user. This development is typical of the do-it-yourself industry, which sells directly to the consumer the product of its research and development services together with the semi-finished good, instead of selling the good ready for consumption in the traditional trade channels. The same reasoning can be applied to leasing which substitutes for the direct sale of machinery and equipment. These are phenomena of *externalization* of services, to which correspond reverse phenomena of *internalization* reflecting the particular development of technology in other fields. As will be seen below, other factors, particularly ones institutional in character, may influence the direction of these changes.

Services Traded at a Distance and Services Furnished on Site

The last important distinction to be made is between services which enter into distant commerce and those which enter only into local commerce. A particular case is that of services which enter into international trade as opposed to services which are only sold on the internal market of a given economic entity. A similar distinction exists for goods, but in this case it is less precise because in principle a good can always be exported or imported. In fact, when theorists of international trade speak of products that do not enter into international trade or nontradable products, they usually refer mainly to services. The problem is that it is wrong to assimilate the bulk of services to nontradable products at the international level. A great number of services can be either sold at a distance (for example, banking or information services) or exchanged through the transfer of support materials in which they are, so to speak, incorporated (printed text containing the result of research work, reports of consultants, cinematographic film, etc.).

Services that do not directly enter into international or distant trade (other than primary services, but more will need to be said about the role of capital) are those which can only be supplied on site, that is, where there is a direct contact between producer and consumer. Examples are expert consulting services (engineering, after-sales service, etc.) retail trade (except mail order houses), personal care such as hairdressing and beauty care, stage shows not otherwise transmitted, restaurant and hotel services, as well as the majority of nonmarket services, such as police, etc. In order for these services to be the subject of an export or an import, the consumer must move to the place of production or vice versa.[4]

Main Types of Services and Their Classification

In order to better determine the relationships between different types of services, table 2–1 presents a classification of the main activities of this sector in terms of the criteria defined above. These activities are distributed as follows (with the categories, classes, or groups corresponding to the International Classification by Industry of all Branches of Economic Activity (ISIC) of the United Nations given in parentheses):

1. Ocean and coastal water transport (7121), air (7131), and land (711) transport.
2. Supporting services to land, water, and air transport (7116, 7123, 7132).

3. Services incidental to transport, e.g., forwarding, packing, brokers, etc. (7191); storage and warehousing (7192).
4. Insurance and reinsurance (82).
5. Financial services: banks, other credit institutions, security dealers, foreign exchange dealers, consultants (81).
6. Business services: legal (8321); accounting, auditing, and bookkeeping (8322); engineering, architectural, and technical services, management services, employment agencies, etc. (8324, 8329); advertising (8325).
7. Data processing and communication services (8323, 7200).
8. Machinery and equipment rentals and leasing (1120, 5000, 6200, 71, 8330, 9490).
9. Construction (5000).[5]
10. Real estate.
11. Wholesale and retail trade (61, 62), restaurants and hotels (63).
12. Repair services (951), laundry services and dry cleaning (952).[5]
13. Recreational and cultural services (94), including motion picture production, distribution, and projection (9411, 9412), radio and television broadcasting (9413).
14. Domestic and personal services (953, 9591, 9599), photography (9592).
15. Public administration (92, 96)[6], sanitary and social and related community services (92, 93), including education services (9130) and research and scientific institutes.

Some would argue that tourism should also be included as a separate category of activity. However, the notion of tourism covers sales not only of services but also of goods to consumers domiciled a certain distance away from the place of consumption. In the context of a national economy, tourism represents a simple displacement of consumer demand to certain specific points in the internal market. The expenses made for goods and services in the place of temporary residence are in general not separately accounted for in national statistics. Even if they were, it would in any event be difficult to distinguish between the expenses made for such and such a service or such and such a good by local consumers and by other consumers, except perhaps in regard to hotel expenses and other specific instances. It is therefore difficult to see why tourism should be considered a service *sui generis*. If it is sometimes presented as such in discussions of international trade, it is because balance-of-payments statistics do not show the precise destination of the expenses of foreign consumers which cover both purchases of goods and services. These expenses are therefore classified among so-called "invisible" transactions which are associated with the notion of service. Hence tourism tends to be considered as a service, but we shall not follow this trend here.

There are three other international payment flows which are sometimes assimilated with service activities *sui generis*, but which we shall not consider as such for our purposes. These are three items of the current account balance labelled "wages, salaries, and other labor income," "interests, dividends, and other income from capital," and "workers' remittances." In the first and third cases as well as in part of the second case (interests), these flows represent all or part of the payment for primary services (labor and capital) which can be used either in the production of services or in the production of goods. For their part, dividends and other income from capital represent in most cases benefits earned abroad by branches or affiliates of enterprises of the reporting country, whatever their type of activity. It would therefore be wrong to consider that these flows are exclusively related to services.

Nevertheless, concerning this last point it will be noted that the importance of invisible transactions in the balance of payments of many countries is often related to the magnitude and diversity of service activities of the enterprises of these countries operating abroad or of foreign enterprises operating on the national territory of the reporting countries. Because services are intangible and generally not transferable from one user to another, in most cases the supplier of the service must be in direct contact with the user in order to be able to perform his activity. The enterprises in question that wish to sell their products on a foreign market need to establish in these markets either directly or indirectly through subsidiaries or affiliates in order to be in touch with the consumer. As a result, a large part of the entries in certain countries' balance of payments under the item *services sold abroad* takes the form of payments for factors or of transfers of profits earned by enterprises which are related in one way or another to the headquarters of firms established in the countries in question. These payments are no different from those made on account of direct or portfolio investments in goods producing enterprises established abroad, except for the fact that service firms have no choice but to adopt this particular form of access to consumers of other countries given the nature of the products they sell.

Specific Aspects of Transactions in Services

Given the above characteristics which are common to many services, economists dealing with the development of international trade in this sector generally include in the notion of trade the activities of service enterprises established abroad, whereas, in the case of goods, they make a clear distinction between international trade in goods and direct investment abroad. The existence of barriers to international trade in goods does in fact confer on investment in the production of goods abroad the character of a substitute for trade, that is, of a means for goods producing firms to avoid or overcome these barriers. For the reasons indicated, it is not possible to make such a clear distinction in the case of services.

For many services, there are no international flows possible because the presence on the place of consumption or use is indispensable. Consequently, services supplied by firms established abroad (particularly when these are supplied directly by personnel originating in the home country) may be considered as exports from the home country, the sole difference with direct sales of services from one country to another being that the factors of production "accompany" the product to the place of consumption.

It is therefore logical to assimilate payment for primary factors used in the production of services abroad on behalf of national enterprises, as well as the repatriation of profits of service enterprises earned abroad, to exports of services, because the motivations for the investments in question are not the same as in the case of goods, and the barriers to *trade* in services properly speaking are not, perforce, a usual means of protection. *Insofar as flows corresponding to each category of service considered on its own can be identified*, the elements of the three items of the balance of payments mentioned under the preceding subtitle may therefore be taken into account as part of national production of services.

Note in passing that the fact of having to establish abroad to develop their activities instead of selling their products across the borders make producers of services relatively more vulnerable than producers of goods to restrictions imposed internally by foreign governments to the exercise of their activities. The regulations concerning investment, establishment, employment, and foreign exchange, to name only the most important ones, have much more impact on international competition in the sector of services, where obstacles to trade per se play a small role, than they do in the goods sector. Moreover, the importance for many services of capital movements on one hand and movements of consumers on the other, in lieu of movements of products, impinges on the prospects for the development of service activities at the international level and therefore on the evolution of productive structures in advanced economies in the so-called postindustrial era.

The analysis of these specific aspects of trade in services should permit the elaboration of new principles of the theory of international trade adapted to modern structures of production and trade. Thus it is clear that the nontransferable character of services influences the economic conditions of supply since the role of distant trade is reduced in consequence. Moreover, because services are heterogeneous by nature both at the level of supply (quality of the service supplied) and level of demand (specificity of needs), the attainment of scale economies, which implies a minimum degree of standardization of the product, is less easy than in the case of goods.

Nevertheless, it is possible to supply minimum service functions which are homogeneous and which correspond to a general demand for essential services of the nonstorable variety. Such services are produced with unskilled, low-paid labor in cyclical unemployment. In international trade, only countries which are able to supply such a labor force may have a comparative advantage in the services in question based on their particular endowment in primary factors of production.

Even in this case, it will be noted that it is not the availability of primary factors that gives rise to a basic advantage in trade, but rather the control over knowledge and advanced techniques in the fields of production and distribution. A case in point is fast-food restaurants. The farther away the markets are from the base where the activities of design and organization are established, the more the scientific, technical, and methodological content of their services plays a crucial role in determining the possibility of expanding the scale of activity. International competition in the area of services is essentially based on such factors, and the "comparative" advantage that certain countries have in trade of services (including production of such services in foreign territory) is often nothing more than an absolute advantage based on their lead in the fields of R&D and O&M (organization and method).

Another aspect of trade of services which deserves special attention is the fact that an important part of the value added of many goods entering international trade consists in services (table 1–1). This means that the whole body of theory of international trade in goods which abstracts from the supply and demand of services incorporated in such goods may lead to misleading conclusions concerning the elements that determine international trade and payments flows between countries.[8] The impact of barriers to trade in goods on the supply and demand of services incorporated in such goods, or which are complementary to them or substitutes for them, should therefore be taken into account in evaluating the effects of these obstacles on the distribution of economic activity between the country or customs territory concerned and foreign or third countries or territories.

These considerations lead to a re-examination of the notion of barrier to trade currently in use as being a simple obstacle to the movement of goods between different countries or customs territories. They bring out the fact that, in practice, obstacles such as customs tariffs or quantitative restrictions

applied at the border and which appear not to affect services because they
are both invisible and intangible, have much more complex effects than
appear at first sight. Conversely, obstacles to trade in services (flag discri-
mination in maritime shipping, restrictions to the freedom of insurance,
etc.) may be considered as nontariff barriers to trade in goods.

With regard to comparative advantage, it should be stressed that countries which do not think that they have a strong competitive ability in the
field of services have, nevertheless, an interest in seeing the development of
efficient service activities at the international level, insofar as these activities
are important inputs into their industrial or agricultural production. Of
relevance in this connection is the distribution and marketing of primary
commodities and semi-processed goods: commodity exchanges, merchant-
ing, transport, insurance, advertising, and wholesale trade. By limiting the
expansion opportunities of these activities, the countries in question may
indirectly reduce their own expansion possibilities in sectors of physical
production. It should be recognized, however, that the technological gap
faced by these countries in the field of services could be filled through the
transfer of technologies from advanced countries, accompanied by sufficient
protection of their internal market to ensure the development of corresponding national services activities economically viable (see chapter 4).

Missing Links in Economic Theory and New Bases of Analysis

To this day, economic theory has only analyzed productive activities from
the point of view of *quantitative* relationships between measurable factors,
deliberately ignoring any indefinite elements such as the intrinsic quality of
products, the social behavior of economic agents, the cultural environment,
and other such influences which have been lumped together in the category
of *external economies or diseconomies*. The study of services, on the contrary, brings to the fore a much more human dimension of economic activity
which may modify the traditional way of looking at production relationships. For example, the fact that services only contain as much value as
there is quality in the performance of the service provider—in other words,
that their utility rests entirely in the manner in which they are provided—
raises doubts about the validity of the criteria used to establish wages and
salary scales in producing enterprises. Indeed, these scales are generally
established on the basis of the assumed objective contribution of different
categories of functions to given physical increments of output. On the other
hand, payment of economic agents on the basis of subjective criteria of
productivity, characteristic of many types of services, may constitute a fair-

er, though more unequal, basis of distribution of the gains from growth.

In fact, the service society is the society of intelligence and talent, and its principal production factor is human capital. Next to this, the notion of labor in the etymological as well as the practical sense of the word loses significance, since the hand of the worker is no longer the essential tool of production which it was in the workshop, on the worksite, or on the farm of the last century. As services activities play an increasingly important role in total output, there is a growing need for the revaluation of tasks in favor of those which the industrial society considered as unproductive because they did not result in the direct creation and accumulation of physical goods.

The next stage in this reasoning consists in questioning the Marxist notion of value based on the accumulation of *elementary* human effort, as well as the Marshallian notion of value based on the marginal utility of the consumer. The basis for this is that these two theories aim at defining the value of products in quantitative terms, whereas for services qualitative criteria of value are needed.[9]

Marxist theory is not applicable to services because small portions of elementary work do not add up to qualified service work. The degree of qualification of service work must be evaluated directly from indices of achievement of a given service activity. It is only when so evaluated that it can serve as a basis for the evaluation of the intrinsic value of a particular service provided. In Marshallian theory, marginal utility as the basis of value is understood in its *objective* meaning of a quantitative adaptation of real demand (financially solvent demand) for each particular product to the increase in the number of such products available on the market. In the case of services, this notion of marginal utility cannot apply because the consumer is almost never faced with the same product. Indeed service acts differ from one performance to another so that in general there is no additionality between services of a same type, and the marginal utility curve is discontinuous.

From the point of view of the organization of production, there are also notable differences between the supply of goods and the supply of services. The division of labor makes possible the reduction of the different phases of the goods-production process to simple and repetitive movements which are totally dissociated from the object being produced: this is characteristic of work on an assembly line. Such a dissection of the act of production is much more difficult to achieve in many services because they are not linked to the utilization of machines. Mechanized services (for example, dry cleaning and fast-food restaurants) are the exception precisely because they separate the most elementary movements from the rest of the service act as in traditional assembly lines.

For other services, the quality of the total service act depends in large measure on the quality of the individual acts of all the agents participating in the production because the repetitive portion of the movement is minimal compared to the creative portion for each service product delivered. One can clearly see this in the case of all services provided by the professions either to business or to the public, in the case of computer services, of traditional retail trade services, of certain transport and insurance services, of most financial services, domestic services, personal services, recreation services, and even public administration.

Such a working relationship necessarily brings about a closer cooperation between all productive agents which, in turn, implies a greater contribution of the individual toward the collective effort in which he/she participates. As a result, there is greater flexibility of management, as well as more direct participation of all employees, and these permit the preservation and improvement of the overall quality of the product by stimulating the provision of quality service acts by each productive agent. Without carrying this reasoning too far, it can be said that in most service activities the collectivization of work rests on the co-responsibility of all productive agents, which in turn leads to a certain equalization of working conditions and status among the various agents. This contrasts with goods production where collectivization results in separating the productive agents in different categories according to the more or less elementary and repetitive character of the tasks entrusted to them. The responsibility of most agents toward the final product is limited to the performance of tasks where their personalities do not intervene. In this sector, it is therefore normal for different categories of productive agents to entertain more antagonistic relationships than in the sector of services.

The modernization of working methods achieved thanks to technology affects in the first place the repetitive tasks which do not require any particular skill. These are simplified and sometimes completely substituted for by machines and instruments. As a result, the workers assigned to these tasks lose the professional status which they had before the appearance of machines. A middle-level rank in the production hierarchy at a prior stage of development becomes a minimum level of qualification later on, leaving to the personnel concerned the choice of accepting a definitive degrading of their position or improving their training in order to recover the rank which they occupied previously in the professional hierarchy. This devaluation of knowledge, already referred to by Marx [1952a, pp. 112–113; also Gustafsson, 1979, p. 25], is a permanent phenomenon linked to technological progress.

It is precisely this link which must be kept in mind when examining the role of services in less-developed economies. Economists used to dealing with the structures of industrial societies are tempted to consider as a form of disguised unemployment the nonqualified services that exist in abundance in developing countries, particularly in the sectors of trade and of personal and domestic services. However, it is not proven that the intensity of use of labor, given its average level of qualification, is higher in the sector of services as a whole in these countries than in semi-industrialized or industrialized countries. Taking into account that the division of labor between services and goods varies according to the level of technological development, it is not demonstrated, either, that the role of services in national production is on the whole more important in developed countries than elsewhere (see chapter 5). The apparent increase in the share of services in the national product of developed countries is probably as much a function of the rapid development of certain traditional services as independent activities, as it is of the development of new service activities.

Nevertheless, the development of new activities is the one factor that conditions the global competitiveness of industrial economies insofar as it confers upon them a "new comparative advantage" at a time when they are losing such advantage to countries in the Third World in certain branches of industry.[10] The content of this advantage can be defined in terms of human capital, either in the form of technical and scientific training or in the form of organizational and management talents acquired during a century and a half of industrial discipline. The possibility to exploit this advantage will, however, depend on the prospects for the development of trade in services and on the possibility of direct access to services markets, either between industrial countries themselves or among these countries and developing countries. This problem, which is currently being discussed in specialized international agencies, will be examined in more detail in chapter 4.

Contribution to the Theory of Postindustrial Development

On the basis of available information, that is, in light of the rapid development of service activities in modern societies and of the role of services in traditional societies (see chapter 5), it seems possible to outline a theory of postindustrial development on the basis of the three following postulates:

1. Work = accumulated knowledge = culture;
2. Services = communication, information;
3. Complementarity of services and goods = compatibility between manual labor and intellectual labor, between hardware and software.

Work as a Cultural Activity

Postulate (1) aims at eliminating the traditional barrier between "productive" and "unproductive" labor and between goods (the fruits of productive labor) and services (the fruits of unproductive labor). It is, however, more far-reaching. It aims at eliminating the distinction between "those who work" and "those who do not work" and between "producers" and "consumers," insofar as this distinction implies that only those activities exercised by economic agents at a stage preceding the sale of a good or of a service bring a positive contribution to the creation of welfare. If, on the contrary, one considers work as the application of accumulated knowledge to practical ends or for practical purposes—in other words, as a simple mode of expression of culture—it then becomes synonymous with creative activity whatever the place or the time at which the work is performed. Thus, the consumer can contribute to the valorization of goods which he acquires in the market and can perform productive tasks with the assistance of these goods. For example, if he buys a piece of furniture in spare parts far from his home, he gives value to the product by transporting it to his place of residence, and he participates in the manufacture of the product by assembling its parts. Similarly, when he helps himself to petrol at the pump station or when he mows his lawn, he accomplishes productive tasks. However, his contribution is not counted as part of national product, whereas it would be in economies where "self-service" does not exist, for the simple reason that the corresponding services would, in the first case, be internalized by the furniture-producing firms (handicraft or industrial) and, in the second case, would be performed by independent agents or service firms (gardeners or service-station attendants).

Thus, work as a source of creation of value is more and more absent from the statistical records on which rest the notions of growth and progress inherited from the materialist theories of the nineteenth century. On the other hand, work is more and more a form of cultural expression which reflects new types of organization of productive forces and new modes of distribution of wealth, wherein the consumer plays a large role in the creation and maintenance of his own well-being through his direct action *as a consumer* and no longer only as a producer.

This reasoning converges with that of Orio Giarini [1980], who has formulated a concept of global material well-being according to which the total value produced in an economy (the sum of "utilization values" of goods and services) is subdivided between monetized and nonmonetized values. The latter includes "free" natural resources (land, water, etc.). Since all products are considered from the point of view of the services they provide, each one of them represents a "stock of services" which includes all these components, and the sum total of these individual stocks represents the Dowry and Patrimony (D&P) of humanity (or of a given society). Work as we have defined it above can be assimilated to a "stock of services" which includes all traditional activities considered as unproductive, but excludes the services provided by natural resources such as air, water, mineral resources, and other "free goods."

The reason for excluding gifts of nature from the notion of stock of services or of work is that natural resources are only of interest to mankind insofar as they can be exploited for man's own well-being. A river is nothing more than a difficult obstacle to cross as long as the arts of fishing or navigation or the use of hydraulic forces are unknown. The sun is no more than a source of heat and light as long as one has not discovered agriculture or learned to capture and transform solar energy. Across centuries entire populations have lived on territories whose soil contained huge mineral resources without having the slightest knowledge of their existence or utility. Gifts of nature are not only free, they are useless for whoever has not discovered their utility through work. Being useless,their conservation is of no interest: a population which has not learned to swim or to navigate has no use for aquaculture and is not concerned about the pollution of the seas. Consequently, rather than attribute an intrinsic value to the gifts of nature as Giarini does, it is appropriate to recognize that these only acquire value thanks to work services which transform and exploit them. However, the value thus acquired is not necessarily a marketable one. It can be an intrinsic value resulting from a series of various creative activities considered as a single whole, such as the value represented by law and order or morality, or by an urban or country landscape. It is therefore the means set in motion by man to control his natural environment, rather than the given features of this environment, which deserve priority attention.[12]

By extrapolating these concepts, we end up turning upside down the moral values and the principles governing individual and collective action on which rested the process of capitalist industrialization in the West. Paradoxically, this reversal of values is the direct consequence of the technical progress made possible by industrialization itself. The definition of work in a way that stresses the *cultural* content (intelligence and experience) of all creative activity results in assigning a primary role, in the hierarchy of human activities, to those which make use of a maximum amount of knowledge, intelligence, imagination, and ingenuity over those which use only their physical force and natural gifts. Just like the priest, the architect, or the scribe of ancient times, the scientist, the researcher, the engineer, and the specialist in electronics nowadays perform the most respected, if not always the best-paid, jobs. Research and scientific and technical training are more important than physical production from which they help man to free himself. Organization and management are more important than applied mechanical science. In short, the greater the "services" content of an activity, the more useful it is and the more respectful it makes those who exercise it. The converse was true in materialist societies undergoing a phase of quantitative expansion such as ancient Rome at the time of the Empire, Europe in the nineteenth century, or a large number of contemporary societies of the Third World, where the manufacturer and the trader hold first rank in society.

The recent evolution of productive structures in industrial societies gives rise to visions of the future which differ from those of the last century. Just as we witness the accelerated robotization of the most repetitive and least creative tasks in the field of material production, we witness the mechanization of the most elementary knowledge, which is reduced to simple elements of information or "bits" by the computer. These elements are part of the store of common knowledge whose sum total is too enormous to be accumulated in the human brain, and which in any event is only of interest as background information for analysis. The mechanization of knowledge, or at least of its most commonplace elements, frees the intellect for more complex tasks, that is, tasks with a higher cultural content, just as robots free the hands of the worker. It also permits the saving of *time* which is an indispensable ingredient of all activities freed from the constraints of the natural environment.[13] Consequently, it makes it possible to envisage the emergence of societies where an increase in leisure will, in and of itself, bring about an increase in the total productivity of the economy.[14]

Services as Functions of Communication and Information

Services confer value onto physical goods by establishing a link between the producer and the market where the producer sells his output. *This elementary function of communication is the foundation of the economic value of services*, as we shall see in chapter 3. It operates directly and concretely in various ways such as transportation or different forms of intermediation: traders, shippers, merchanters, customs agents, advertisers, bankers, insurers, etc. In reality, almost all traditional services perform this function. Thus, if services are divided into two categories,[15] those that are linked in one way or another to the sale of merchandise and those that are not, we note that the majority belong to the first category. In the second category, there are a number of intermediary services which play a role in production while not contributing directly to the manufacture of goods (accounting services, design and applied research services, administrative and rental services) and, especially, consumption services (rental, recreation, domestic, and personal services).

Just like material production, communication has progressed, thanks to an ever greater division of labor, to technical progress and to the gradual assimilation of improved methods of organization and management. Services have correspondingly become speedier and more reliable. They have become richer in content from the experience acquired through centuries of development of a market economy first on a national, then on a continental and global, scale, particularly since the industrial revolution.[16, 17] This quantitative increment in content has finally resulted in a notable improvement in their quality. To illustrate the point, one need only compare today's banking, insurance, accounting, design, research services, etc., to what they were in eighteenth century Europe. They have evolved *pari passu* with the improvement in the quality of work, as has material production itself.

However, there is in this regard a difference of nature between services and goods. The latter embody indirectly the progress achieved in the content of work, whereas services which have no physical support express these improvements directly, in their very essence, that is to say, in the manner in which they are rendered. The cultural content of work is transmitted directly to the agent delivering the service to the consumer, instead of being embodied in an inert, destructible object. Services, therefore, fulfill an *information function* while being themselves made up of a set of accumulated lessons of experience.

The information acquired and transferred by economic agents in the sector of services is more or less evenly distributed among them and can in extreme cases be controlled by a small number of individuals. Just as the engineer and the factory manager understand better than the worker the significance of the latter's manual tasks, the director of an airline company is better informed than the air-hostess about the running of his business. However, because the role of the simple employee is much more important in the case of services due to the fact that he/she is in direct contact with the consumer, information on the purposes and modalities of the service rendered as well as on the economic context in which it is being provided tends to be better distributed in this sector than in industry.

Not only information in general (acquired or accumulated) but also information of the economic agents (shared with a view to be more efficiently transmitted) are to services what raw materials are to goods production. The cult of information which is a characteristic of advanced industrial societies thus essentially reflects the rapid development of service activities in those societies.

The historical process leading to the progressive transformation of modern economies into "information societies" can be schematically described as follows:

1. Industrialization,
2. Capitalization of production,
3. Search for economies of scale,
4. Widening of the market,
5. Need for better links between production of goods and the market,
6. Development of service activities,
7. Increasing need for information,
8. Emergence of the information society.

The information society is characterized: (1) at the intellectual level by the accumulation and conservation of data (data banks) and by the development of knowledge through study and analysis (fundamental research, applied sciences, software); (2) at the physical level by the development of techniques for the processing (computer) and the communication of data (telematics).

Hardware and Software

It is not easy to push the above reasoning to the limits of philosophy, as one could be tempted to do in trying to bring together all the constituent elements of creative activity. We shall nevertheless take that risk, since in any case the study of service activities necessarily leads to taking a new look at the finality of economic activity.

The observed complementarity between services and goods, their undissociable character, is a logical consequence of the definition of work in terms of cultural content. Beyond complementarity, it is appropriate to try and understand how far manual and intellectual labor, or what in modern language we call hardware and software, are compatible. Compatibility implies that the two types of activities are subjected to the same operational rules and are governed by the same principle, i.e., the principle of multidimensional *concretization* of the purposes of human activity—call it progress, development, or civilization.

The principle of concretization, which is the motive force behind the information society, realizes the synthesis between knowledge and action.

Now, this principle is markedly different from the efficiency principle (should we not from now on speak of the myth of efficiency?) which has governed industrial societies from the outset. The efficiency principle is based on a purely quantitative evaluation of output (volume, weight, number, market value), practically ignoring quality which in any case is not measurable with the indicators chosen. Efficiency is measured by the relation between output and cost, both expressed in concrete parameters whose interaction can be expressed in mathematical language. On the contrary, the net result of work as defined above (as opposed to the net output of "productive" labor in the Smithian definition) is for a large part evaluated in qualitative and, hence, abstract terms.[18]

The immediate consequence of this approach is the acceptance of a certain economic cost to preserve cultural heritage and enrich it. In welfare economics this is referred to as the social cost of activities whose pursuit is not necessarily justified from the point of view of efficiency as measured by the quantitative return from the factors employed. In addition, it can be stated that the fact that compatibility can be restored between intellectual and manual labor in no way diminishes the recognized superiority of intellectual over manual labor, save for the fact that this superiority is not based on the nature of the work performed but only on the greater cultural content of intellectual labor in the majority of cases. On the other hand, where the cultural content of manual labor is greater than that of intellectual labor, the hierarchy is necessarily reversed: the work of the watchmaker is more valuable than that of the typist.

In a society where such a new hierarchy of work is established and where at the same time the traditional simplistic distinction between intellectual and manual labor tends to disappear, life can no longer be organized in terms of the sole criterion of physical productivity, as it still is in semi-industrialized and newly industrialized societies. In fact, in countries where industrialization has followed the capitalist model, the emerging information society is faced with social relations which are much more organized that they were in the initial phase of industrialization. This organization is the result of the conflicts of interest which characterize the capitalist mode of physical production based on workshop discipline. In the long run, it evolves into a necessary dialogue between employers on one hand and employees and workers on the other, which is the first stage toward a closer cooperation between individuals in the work place. This cooperation develops in step with the cultural content of work, and it improves as the final outcome of the productive process depends more and more on the personal contribution of each factor of production. Thus, in any little developed service activity, the relation of subordination between managers and operating staff cannot reach the level of depersonalized automatism which was characteristic of early industrial relations.

New society, old structures

The preceding observations present a somewhat idealized picture of the end result of an evolutionary process which, in fact, started fairly recently toward new forms of productive activity solely composed of services, as well as toward a new division of labor between physical and intangible production. In the present transition period, production is still very largely organized along traditional lines. There is a clear division of responsibility between business entrepreneurs and managerial staff who are in possession of information, and operating staff to whom information is communicated bit by bit and only to the extent necessary to permit it to fulfill the specific tasks which are assigned to it.

The quality of services rendered suffers from this lack of communication, particularly in sectors of activity where the cultural content of work is high, because the work performed in those sectors improves with the knowledge of the context in which it takes place. For example, in public administration, banking, brokerage, data processing, research, etc., information of the agents on the business situation of their enterprise and on the external factors which affect it conditions the quality of their contribution to the attainment of the objectives of the enterprise. This is even beginning to be the case for factory work. For example, the near-abolition of assembly lines in the Swedish automobile industry has had positive results on average output per worker.

The persistence of traditional methods of organization of work in the sector of services reflects an old quantitative concept of productivity based on the number of units produced by unit of expenditure (unit cost). The application of this concept to services leads to the standardization of such service acts as lend themselves to some drastic form of simplication, obtained by removing from the services concerned a large part of their cultural content. Thus, for example, it is possible to create a large number of units of food catering services by reducing each unit to the simplest possible form and supplying it through a chain of restaurants where only standardized dishes are served for quick snacks. However, only a small number of elementary services can be dealt with in this way.

It has often been observed that developing countries have at least as much difficulty in assimilating the methods of work of industrialized countries as they have in assimilating their techniques, and such assimilation has been described as a form of cultural impoverishment. The real reason for this is that traditional societies operate on the basis of a less materialistic outlook on life than capitalist industrial societies. Even though it may be exaggerated to speak of cultural impoverishment, there is at least some acculturation taking place, due to the transformation or outright disappearance of traditional activities and, with them, of the accumulated knowledge that found expression in the work performed by the individuals engaged in these activities. The most notable example is that of handicraft. In the area of services, traditional medicine and meteorology are cases in point.

This phenomenon is interesting for new services societies of the post-industrial era because it shows that there is some incompatibility between industrial organization of work and a broader cultural concept of work. This incompatibility is being felt in the present transition phase toward an information society, no longer as a constraint imposed by technical progress, but as an institutional burden inherited from the past.

Few economists nowadays are interested in studying ways of exploiting the accumulated experience of industrial societies to move the development process forward, but other researchers have devoted attention to this problem. Among them, Aurelio Peccei has argued strongly in favor of a new form of human development which involves rejecting what he calls the "paroxysm of progress" of modern man "trapped by his marvellous successes" [see Peccei, 1981]. François Perroux [1981] follows the same inspiration in presenting an alternative approach to development of the Third World. Without subscribing to the apocalytpic vision of the modern world which is typical of the systematic Cassandrism of the Club of Rome, nor to the obsession with the "biosphere" which haunts the minds of its disciples,[19] it is worth noting that Peccei also underlines the *cultural* aspect of development: ". . . the evolutionary plan (of man) has never been and cannot be to modify his own biology (in order to adapt to his environment). On the contrary, it is to modify his environment, and this forces him to develop continuously" [1981, p. 55].

Later on he says: "Indeed, contemporary society is so polarized on material objectives and problems that its main aim seems to be to teach people how to do things, just things. All education and training are geared to this purpose . . . and yet it is the quality of the protagonist which counts in the saga of mankind. . . " [1981, pp. 115–116].

Although our intention is not to drag the reader into philosophical contemplations on the destiny of mankind or the future of the planet Earth, it is useful to note that the vast panorama of civilization drawn up by Aurelio Peccei forces reflection on the contradictions of societies which are undergoing a process of change such as our own. The postindustrial economy will have to free itself from materialist prejudices in order to make progress. It will have to discover new principles of action better adapted to a mode of production which is more qualitative than quantitative, and which can play the role that the quest for profit played during the period of industrialization. It will have to create structures that (1) favor a dialogue among the various groups of economic agents born of advanced industrial societies; (2) substitute for automatic market mechanisms; and (3) which, paying due attention to the high level of social protection already reached, make full use of the methods of consultation put in place to control the allocation and redistribution of the wealth of nations.

This being said, it should be clear that the contradiction between old structures and new aspirations, which are becoming increasingly apparent in contemporary societies, will not be resolved by returning to an imaginary golden age of the quality of life where each individual can determine his/her own participation in the common effort to improve welfare by reference to a self-centered zero growth criterion. On the other hand, in economies dominated by service activities, it may not be as necessary, as in societies which are engaged in large-scale industrialization processes, to maintain conditions of competition such as are dictated by market mechanisms for goods in the form, for example, of an open-trading system.[20] The advent of the postindustrial era could therefore bring about profound mutations in the institutions that govern national economies as well as international economic cooperation.

At the national level, it is clear that the relations of interdependence will no longer be the same as soon as the production of services definitely supersede the production of goods in the economy. In addition, the relations of interdependence between economies where the production of services is predominant and those where the production of goods is predominant may not evolve harmoniously if based on the principles of free competition and comparative advantage which fit the technical requirements of goods production.

To illustrate, let us consider industrial technology, which is a product of applied research and, therefore, a service activity. In another study, the following comment has been made on this subject: ". . . technology is not a raw material. The accumulation of knowledge which it embodies cannot be easily confiscated by its authors or its priviledged users . . . knowledge being a renewable resource by nature, its dissemination cannot possibly bring about an impoverishment of those who control it. Therefore, the transfer of technology between North and South is essentially an institutional issue, which raises the question whether the State can, and if so how, intervene to stimulate a better and broader dissemination of technical knowledge for the benefit of developing countries and of their enterprises" [Nusbaumer, 1981, p. 165].

The question of the role of the state in international economic relations is therefore likely to be much more crucial than in the previous postindustrial era because the existence of services societies implies a much closer cooperation between service producers and goods producers both inside these societies (given the need to facilitate a synthesis between knowledge and action) and in their relations with the outside world (given the need to facilitate a mutually beneficial exchange of services against goods among trading nations). Thus, one should not lose sight of the fact that the development of service activities takes place at least in part at the cost of a contraction of the industrial sector, were it only as a result of the transfer of industrial activities with a low technological content toward less-developed countries. And, if the industrial base of a country becomes smaller and smaller, its dependence vis-à-vis other goods producing countries increases accordingly. It must therefore rely on these countries, and find bases of agreement with them to guarantee its access to supplies of production goods, intermediate goods, and consumer goods. In general, the intervention of the state is necessary to reach durable solutions in the field of international economic relations.

Such intervention can take various forms. It can either be direct, as advocated by the authors of the New International Economic Order[21] or as practiced by socialist states among themselves, or indirect, operating through a set of contractual rules of conduct which leave considerable scope for the free interplay of market forces.[22] In any case, it is not unreasonable to think that economic relations between countries whose economies are largely service-oriented and those whose economies are still largely dominated by agricultural and industrial production will become more and more intergovernmental in character, given the necessity for governments to play an active role in defining the regulatory framework which will govern the mutual dependence between services producing countries and countries producing essential goods.

The observations above should not be read as an apology of state intervention in relations between countries at different levels of development. However, it is clear that services differ from goods and must consequently be subjected to other rules than those which govern commercial competition and profit. The commercial concept of common price, which applies to goods and which justifies the nonintervention of the state in the free interplay of market forces, does not apply to services except for a limited set of standardized services. This is made clear from the fact that the intolerance threshold above which the economic interpenetration of nations is slowed down by sociological and political factors is, at least initially, lower for services than it is for goods due to the greater cultural content of the former. In this regard, it is enough to mention legal, health, economic, and recreation services, as well as research, education, and management services, and social, community, and artistic services.

In the long run, it may be possible to envisage a greater degree of interpenetration thanks to progress made in the development of communication media, which should facilitate better access to information, a broader dissemination of knowledge, and a certain harmonization of cultures. However, this is likely to be a slow process which naturally meets with strong resistance insofar as it affects life styles and established hierarchies of moral and political values. Any attempt to artificially accelerate the process by unleashing market forces in all sectors of services may be counterproductive.[23]

Technology Transfers

Transfers of technology are the principal means of harmonizing cultures between technology-advanced and industrializing countries. Any encouragement to adapt modern techniques of manufacture to local needs is accompanied by an encouragement to adopt methods of organization and management of work which permit the efficient implementation of these techniques.

Moreover, it is possible to compare the technological recipes which are transferred to encapsulated services produced by the ingenuity and industrial discipline acquired during two centuries of industrialization in advanced countries. The greater the proportion of such service products in the export of advanced countries, the greater the influence of these countries on the modes of development of the countries that import them. And, consequently, the greater is the cultural influence of the suppliers of technology on the latter countries.

This being said, such influence can also be exerted in a much more direct fashion than through the exportation of technological products. Technical assistance supplied to developing countries by specialists operating on the spot, or teachings dispensed to students originating from these countries in the universities of the developed world, constitute a mode of supplying services which is complementary to the transfer of technological products or which substitutes for it.[24] This supply mode provides a further stimulus to the assimilation by host countries of the cultural standards associated with imported techniques of production. In turn, cultural harmonization encourages exports of marketable services in their most direct form, that is, through the establishment of production agents at the place of production.[25]

Economic theory has always considered trade in goods as a substitute for movements of factors of production, except that trade encounters fewer natural obstacles than migrations. It is clear that as far as factors of production are concerned, such "natural" obstacles that exist are cultural in nature. The above considerations point to the fact that services cannot be adapted to cultural differences among their users as easily as goods can because they are carriers of a complex heritage of relationships and values related to the specific experience of the service providers. It is for this reason that services often require the presence of the provider at the place of utilization. Now, in view of the fact that service activities are expanding in advanced countries, these countries will become more and more dependent on exports of such activities. As a result, they could only contemplate with concern the erection of new obstacles to the migration of factors in countries which are net importers of technology and know-how.

These considerations bring us back to a question that has often been raised concerning the development prospects of Third World countries, that is, whether these countries will be in a position to increase their material well-being and accede rapidly to the stage of information societies without undergoing the traumas of the industrial revolution of the nineteenth century. Similar sufferings are already being endured by the population of countries that follow the development model of present-day industrialized countries. The major concern of many economists and other specialists of political science interested in the Third World is therefore to transplant into developing countries, together with modern techniques, the principles governing social organization and distribution of wealth of advanced countries. It is true that this objective is often accompanied by the rejection of the capitalist economic model, but the main point is not the particular political framework chosen to attain it.

The expansion of exchanges of goods against services between industrializing and advanced countries could contribute to the achievement of a smooth transition toward a modern form of society in Third World countries. It would make it possible for the latter to acquire the knowledge necessary to bring within their reach the benefits of less unequal social organization. At the present stage of development of economic, political, and cultural relations at the international level, such considerations remain inevitably somewhat theoretical. However, it should at least be possible to avoid transfers of knowledge being limited to industrial technology, and to facilitate access to all the other constituent elements of the culture of economically advanced countries in the Third World as a whole, while leaving to each country the choice of assimilating or rejecting this or that other aspect of that culture.

Commentary
Wealth, Welfare, and the Hidden Economy

In his report to the Club of Rome entitled *Dialogue on Wealth and Welfare*, Orio Giarini put forward, as indicated above [1980, p. 19], a number of postulates concerning the definition of value and the evaluation of welfare which throw new light on the finality of economic development, notably in regard to the role of certain nonmarketable services which have the characteristics of public goods. In this context, Giarini deals on one hand with the problem of nonmonetized activities and, on the other, with what is commonly known as the "underground," "invisible," or "hidden" economy [Giarini, 1980, especially pp. 116–117, 223–245, and 147–165]. He presents this latter phenomenon as being essentially linked to the monetized sector of the economy and does not distinguish between goods and services supplied by "moonlighting." In this commentary we shall examine successively these two aspects of Giarini's contribution to the evaluation of welfare in order to see to what extent they facilitate an understanding of the role of services in the economy.

Nonmonetized Economic Activities and Ecological Heritage

For Orio Giarini, *"the utilization value of a product or service is built up and guaranteed by a series of monetized activities (costs) . . . and non-monetized activities*, and of stocks of goods and services such as:
- unpaid work,
- qualitative (cultural) accomplishments of individuals,
- free circulation of free goods (e.g., water to wash or drink) derived from the natural and nonmonetized Dowry and Patrimony, related to their life period [1980, p. 155].[26]"

Unpaid work includes activities that result in the creation of goods as well as services activities, properly speaking. The two other categories of nonmonetized activities are pure services. "Qualitative accomplishments" are obtained through the accumulation of knowledge and the application of reasoning or of art or artifacts to this knowledge in order to develop the cultural environment and the social framework in which individuals lead their lives. These accomplishments can be assimilated to public goods such as order, peace, security, and health, but they also include every kind of improvement of human beings in the intellectual and moral sense of the term. The value of "free goods" (nature) is not based on the mere fact that they exist, but on the value of the real or potential services which they provide, given the fact that such services are provided without human intervention and at no cost, as is the case for the air we breathe.[27]

The best examples of unpaid work are the services of housewives or those which the do-it-yourself consumer renders unto himself. Such services can be considered as a form of valorization of time. The economies of time realized by the husband thanks to the work of the housewife allows him to devote more time to produce in the monetized sector of the economy. Assuming that the benefits are equitably shared between the partners, the additional income of the husband adds value to the free time of the spouse insofar as she has no possibility of finding more remunerative employment.

The saving made by the do-it-yourself consumer is effected partly on the price of the good purchased in spare parts instead of fully assembled, partly on the salary of the worker whom he would have had to hire to do the assembly. This saving is what finances the free time he devotes to assembling the good. In both cases, we are dealing with the opportunity cost of production factors.[28] The opportunity cost of the free time of the housewife is nil or so low that it is not worth upsetting the balance of the household for its sake: this is indeed the reason why female labor is in part occasional labor, as the attraction of working outside the home (the opportunity cost of household work) varies with the level of remuneration of the monetized activities that women can undertake. For women whose husbands have a high income and whose earnings from household work are consequently high, there is normally little chance that the opportunity cost of their work will be higher than the return from it (except maybe in the case of women who can exercise a high-skill professional activity). As far as the free time of the do-it-yourself consumer is concerned, save in the case where this type of work is a form of entertainment or hobby, its value arises mainly on the fact that its opportunity cost is low compared to the saving realized on the cost of the final product. Indeed, the return from additional paid work which the do-it-yourself consumer could earn would only cover a small portion of the salary of the worker or craftsman he would have to hire to assemble the product.

In the two preceding examples, unpaid services *substitute* for monetized production of goods or services. It is therefore not possible in such cases to speak of a net creation of value in the form of external economies. For this reason, the unpaid activities in question contribute nothing to global welfare. They can even lead to a reduction of welfare by monopolizing too much of the free time of individuals who could make better use of it by improving their knowledge and productive ability, i.e., to increase the cultural content of the work they perform in the monetized sector of the economy. This conclusion is not, in fact, incompatible with that which Giarini draws from his analysis, since he recognizes implicitly that unpaid work can have a negative impact on welfare when he says: "It is not a question whether 'do-it-yourself' is good or bad but of which *combination* of monetarized activities produces *more* real utilization value" [Giarini, 1980, p. 232].[29] The interest of the above conclusion rests in that it introduces a useful distinction between service activities which do not play a linkage function in the economy (see chapter 3) and those that do. The activities discussed above are in some sense the mirror image of commercial production, and they remain linked to it by their implicitly marketable character.

The debate opened by Orio Giarini on unpaid work is nonetheless interesting from the point of view of the theory of endogenous development in least-developed countries.[30] It brings to light, in the case of services linked to the production of goods, the role of certain nonmarketable, social, and community services which are difficult to define but which can contribute in one way or another to increasing the welfare of the populations concerned, precisely because they are supplementary to, rather than substitutes for, commercial production. It would be a mistake to ignore this type of service when looking for means of improving the standard of living in Third World countries other than by external financial assistance from developed countries. In practice, there are few known examples of activities which can play this sort of supplementary role to physical production, but it is true also that little attention has been devoted to this question up to now.

The second type of nonmonetized activities identified by Giarini, i.e., qualitative or cultural accomplishments of individuals, is related to the notion of cultural content of work. While the version presented by Giarini [1980, pp. 180–184] is directly derived from the notion of development of quality of man propounded by Aurelio Peccei, the description he gives of the process of cultural accumulation could very well apply *mutatis mutandis* to the process of accumulation of knowledge and welfare which determines the distribution between services production and goods production at different stages of economic development (see chapter 5).

The third type of nonmonetized activities consists in the utilization of natural resources supplied freely by nature. The central idea in this case is the progressive depletion of nonrenewable resources and the deterioration of the environment (biosphere or ecosystem). These ecological concerns are beyond the scope of the present study, but they are interesting from the point of view of the definition of services. If we limit ourselves to the definition of services given at the beginning of this chapter, it is impossible to accept the idea that nature could per se be the source of services in the sense of *activities*. Nature is, in fact, neither a source of communication nor a source of information outside the realm of man's work. The biosphere is an inert datum whose economic value is derived solely from such work.

There is, moreover, a logical contradiction between conferring a non-monetized value to cultural development and asserting that nature produces value per se.[31] The destruction in the long run of the ecological heritage, if it really occurs (and this remains to be demonstrated), presents no interest except insofar as human labor must be applied to remedy it. Short-term damage caused by industrialization and the exploitation (that is, not only the overexploitation) of given agricultural potential, are only transient diseconomies for which man quickly learns to compensate through experience. In evaluating the contribution of services to the economy, it is therefore prudent to omit any reference to the so-called services given by earth, water, air, and fire unless one wants to enroll God in the active population of this planet.

Services in the Hidden Economy

An apparently growing portion of productive activities escapes taxes and therefore also fails to appear in the national accounts of industrial countries. These are not, properly speaking, nonmonetized activities, since those who accomplish them are effectively paid. On the contrary, for Orio Giarini, "In certain countries, the grey economy is so extensive and so dynamic that it may be considered to indicate the monetarized economy's need to have growing recourse to this type of disguised subsidy in order to maintain itself as the dominant economic system" [1980, p. 234].

This manner of presenting the problem is, however, very unsatisfactory. The essential characteristic of the invisible economy is not to guarantee at all costs the supremacy of the monetary economy over the subsistence or non-profit economy, as if the latter were a valid alternative to paid interchange in modern societies. While not denying the role that taxes play in the expansion of "moonlighting," the new definition of work emerging from the study of service activities presented in this book authorizes a more optimistic interpretation of the phenomenon. Thus, as goods production becomes more mechanical and automatic, work in the goods production sector is more and more depersonalized. At the same time, progress in education increases the access of individuals to knowledge as well as enhancing their creative faculties. Now, the production structures inherited from the industrial revolution do not give individuals the opportunity to express their personality in their work or to accomplish the "more intelligent" work which they feel suited for thanks to their higher education. Seen from this angle, "black work" or moonlighting, which is almost always performed by individuals, may correspond to a desire to make use of these newly acquired capacities. It can be argued that individuals working in the underground economy would probably, were it not for tax constraints that force them to accept lower remunerations, prefer to devote all their time and effort to this kind of small-firm activity than to carry on working as subordinates in the large manufacturing enterprises where they are officially employed.

While a large part of moonlighting takes place in the goods production sector (including repairs which belong to that sector, according to the classification presented at the beginning of this chapter), many underground activities have the characteristics of consumer services. It is not unreasonable to think that the near disappearance of the category of domestic and personal services from the national accounts statistics of developed countries only serves to conceal the transfer of this category of activity into the underground economy.

Notes

1. However, as will be seen in chapter 3, the opportunity cost of these services is not necessarily lower.
2. The inclusion by the Club of Rome [see Giarini, 1980, p. 155] of natural resources such as land, underground resources, and the elements in the notion of service is an extension of the classical notion of value embodied in land.
3. There are, however, certain border cases such as repairs. Repairs are often classified among services, but given the fact that they are performed on goods for which they modify the structure and the physical properties, they can be considered as constituting primary auxiliary services of the same nature as those performed by factors assigned to the production of goods in their new state.
4. When such physical movements take place they entail a modification and widening of the classical notion of "market" as applied to the marketing of goods, wherein the consumer passively attracts supply and makes his choice between competing goods transported to his place of residence. In fact, the very great mobility of persons between different economic entities, due in particular to the rapid development of tourism, probably no longer justifies conceiving of the market for the services referred to as being contained within narrowly circumscribed geographical limits.
5. This type of service may be considered as belonging to the cycle of manufacturing of goods. It is included here to give a broad view of the activities generally considered as part of the services sector.
6. Government services in the field of legal protection may be deemed to include the protection of inventions and of intellectual innovation through patents and copyrights. Generally speaking, protection and police services provided by governments represent a nonnegligi-

ble contribution, albeit difficult to measure, to the national output of any country (see below and chapter 3).

7. In general services are not storable as such because of their transient, nonrenewable nature. However, information is storable for any civilization that has invented a writing medium. Thus in principle, every service may be considered as reproducible as long as its content in information is reproducible. However, in reality the service provided is only the case-by-case expression of the information acquired by the service provider; it is related to information in the same way that speech is related to thought. Therefore one can conclude that service products or individual service acts can only be produced in large numbers if demand for them is assured, i.e., if they correspond to basic needs.

8. On this point see Tucker [1979, p. 22].

9. This approach corresponds in fact to a technological development which appears irreversible and which progressively eliminates all the elementary tasks on which physical production has always been based. The simplest service functions disappear in the same manner.

10. In this connection see Nusbaumer [1981, p. 109]. The concept of comparative advantage is understood here in its widest acceptation of a particular ability to carry out certain types of activities. In fact, because talent and knowledge are universally available factors, it would be more correct to speak of absolute advantage. Consequently, the notion of competition which underlies the theory of international trade loses its purely commercial meaning, and the theory itself ceases to apply fully to trade in services.

11. See in particular section 2.3 of chapter 2 and the definition of D&P on p. 42. The theories of Giarini are discussed in more detail at the end of this chapter in the Commentary. The words in quotation marks are Giarini's own.

12. In this regard, one can argue, as do certain ecologists, that the cost of protecting or rehabilitating the environment must be deducted from the value of natural resources.

13. "Time is the natural domain of human development," said K. Marx [1952a, p. 107].

14. It should be noted that the emergence of such societies does not depend on the adoption of a new economic system, since it is in fact the advanced capitalist societies which are closest to that model.

15. Although we will not examine them in detail here, it should be noted that there are nonmarketable services in both categories.

16. See Jacques Ruffié [1982]: ". . . how many poor, underdeveloped countries could employ to their greatest advantage the managers whom we push into early retirement and who could bring them the technology they so badly need! These men represent an invaluable asset which is being completely squandered."

17. On the preindustrial era, see I. Wallerstein [1980].

18. Note the analogy between this reasoning and the results of the econometric analysis of long-term trends of production by Abramowitz [1], Kuznets [42], and Denison [26], for whom residual values represent "advance in knowledge, [which] is the biggest and most basic reason for the persistent long-term growth of output per unit of input. . . . It includes what is usually defined as technological knowledge and also "managerial knowledge". . . . Advances in knowledge comprise knowledge originating in this country and abroad, and knowledge obtained in any way: by organized research, by individual research workers and inventors, and by simple observation and experience."

19. For a critical analysis of the ecological postulates of the Club of Rome, see *infra*.

20. To illustrate, it may be recalled that protection through patents and copyrights has always been considered, even in the most liberal economic systems, as a necessary form of assistance to invention or intellectual or artistic creation. For a theoretical analysis of the role of patents, see Plant [1934].

21. Resolution adopted by the United Nations General Assembly in March 1974, which Third World countries have used as their main source of argument in their relations with the industrialized North.

22. In this respect, see the book by Ronald K. Shelp [1981], particularly the last two chapters.

23. The frontiers of interdependence are constantly receding, but it has taken centuries to move from the horizon of the village to that of the world economy. See Wallerstein [1980] and Braudel [1979].

24. "The transfer of knowledge and skills has shown itself to be one of the principal characteristics of tradable services. In some sectors this transfer is minimal (e.g., transportation or tourism), while in others such transfer is the main value of the service" [Task Force on Trade in Services, Background Report, Ottawa, October 1982, p. 24].

25. On all these phenomena and the dependency that results for the Third World, see Samir Amin [1973].

26. The words in italics are underlined in the original. The terminology used in this Commentary is sometimes different from Giarini's own, some of it being drawn from the French translation of his book. The D&P is defined by Giarini as "the stock of natural, biological and man-made goods and services we have available to us and from which we derive our welfare in the largest sense of the term [that is] including the stock of goods produced without *any* human intervention, i.e., the earth with its water, air and different climates, and a certain number of biological assets" [1980, p. 42].

27. See above and below for criticisms of this aspect of the theory of D&P.

28. This is, of course, only one of several methods of evaluating unpaid work, as has been clearly demonstrated by L. Goldschmidt-Clermont [1982], but it is the method best adapted to the definition of services (quality and specificity) given in the present study.

29. The words in italics are underlined in the original. It may be noted, however, that Giarini only gives explicit recognition to the phenomenon of negative value-added (or deducted value) in the sphere of ecology.

30. On this point, see François Perroux [1981] and the publications of the *Fondation internationale pour un autre développement* (2, place du Marché, Nyon, Switzerland).

31. That is, according to Kant, independently of human knowledge.

3 VALUE AND COST OF SERVICES

Almost everything which economists have written to this day on services is based on incomplete and even incoherent statistics and on inappropriate methods of analysis. Only a few of them have pointed to these deficiencies and to the directions in which research should be oriented in order to remedy them. There is now a greater, albeit only emerging consciousness of the need to find ways of measuring more precisely the value of service products and productivity in the services sector, and this justifies the hope that an improved understanding of realities will gradually be gained in the process. It will probably be necessary to revise a large number of theories of the contribution of services to economic growth and development, as well as of their role in international trade—in other words, of their contribution to the adjustment of production structures in response to modifications of the international competitiveness of firms. The subject is complicated not only because it is largely unexplored but also because it requires shedding certain habits of thought which are linked to the all-too-familiar idea that physical production is the source of all value. The solutions proposed in the present chapter should not, therefore, be considered as anything more than a first attempt to open the way toward a better understanding of the effective contribution of services to the development of society. Much research must still be carried out before reliable answers can be given to all the questions that arise in this connection.

The problem of measurement of the value produced by services has two aspects. The first and general aspect relates to the evaluation of the "real" value-added in different sectors or subsectors of activities, in a way which corresponds more or less to the notion of real value produced in the form of goods. The task consists in evaluating the quantity or "volume" of products obtained, taking into account, as much as possible, changes in the quality of the products concerned. This is a classical problem, as is the debate on whether the traditional method of deflating current values by prices takes quality changes sufficiently into account. It is all the more difficult to solve in the field of services since the notion of quantity of service is very vague, but it is not specific to this sector. A number of solutions have been proposed in order to better identify in the case of services the element of welfare creation inherent in any form of production,[1] but these solutions remain within the bounds of the traditional intellectual framework which underlies conventional methods of national accounting.

The second aspect of the measurement problem is specific to services, since it consists in identifying units of the product and of defining the equivalence between the sum of the units and the total volume or total value of the output. Few economists have given consideration to this purely microeconomic aspect of the production of services, since in general the preoccupation has rather been to evaluate statistically the global role of services in gross national product (GNP) and their relationship to growth.[2]

The present chapter will be mainly devoted to this second aspect of the problem. A review of the main attempts made to date to find objective indicators of value produced in services will show that the approaches based on methods of estimating goods production are not always fully satisfactory, for the simple reason that they are derived from a quantitative concept of output and its corollary, the common market price, both of which are less applicable to services than they are to goods. It will therefore be necessary, so to speak, to go back to the origins of economic reasoning in order to free ourselves from the tracks laid down by two centuries of what François Perroux has called "mechanist" economic theories [Perroux, 1981, pp. 142ff].

Calculation of the Value of a Service Product

It can be seen from an inventory of the various ways in which value-added in services has been expressed that there is a multiplicity of indicators in use, the same activity being often described from different angles in order to apprehend its essential characteristics; yet, no single indicator gives a precise idea of the content of each activity. This contrasts with the uniqueness of each object in which the value of the good is embodied, a uniqueness which makes it possible to clearly identify the services rendered by the good by referring to the object itself.

There are certain services whose market value can be determined by referring to a good which supports or carries this value—for example, an artbook or a gramophone record—but the value of the majority of services can only be estimated on the basis of statistics relating to the market value of subsets of acts performed, considered as representative of the contribution of the services in question to the total output of a given economic entity.

Some conventional subsets provide an overall evaluation of the receipts of service enterprises or individual service producers; for example, net interests received by banks or total sales of retail outlets. When individual service acts are used as a basis of evaluation, the units correspond to units of final consumption (a medical examination, a concert, a haircut, etc.). The production of services is sometimes calculated as a residual value of GNP, after deduction of industrial, handicraft, and agricultural production. However, in every case the relationship between the value of the services provided and their cost of production is difficult to determine, because precise information on the *quantity* (number of units) of service supplied by unit of factor employed is not available. It is for this reason that the method of "double deflation" which consists of dividing the value of inputs and outputs by appropriate price indices in order to obtain "real" value-added is rarely utilized to calculate the production of services.

The examples shown in table 3–1 give an idea of the variety of production indicators utilized in the sector of services. The table illustrates the lack of precision available on the nature of the acts performed, in contrast to goods production where one at least knows the nature and the number of goods produced, even if one is not always very well informed about their respective qualities. How much more difficult, then, it is to apply a general theory of value to services! Indeed, what sense do concepts like "embodied work" or "marginal utility" have when the units of the product are not distinct?

In effect, this difficulty only gives a very sketchy idea of the complexity of the problem. Due to the obsession with physical production which underlies existing economic theories, there is a natural inclination to look for everything which makes a service resemble a thing, whereas in reality a service should be considered as an *act*.[3] Such an act is somewhat similar to the act of working which is at the origin of all things men use, but its value can only be defined indirectly, through the *valorization* of goods which it makes possible

Table 3–1. Examples of Indicators Used to Calculate the Volume of Production of Services[1]

Type of Activity	"Unit" of Product	Indicators of Value of Production	Deflator
Hairdressing services	Permanent wave, etc.	Gross turnover at current prices	Price index for haircut, permanent wave, etc.
Medical services	Medical examination, work day in the hospital	Number of visits, of work days, amount of sickness insurance premiums	Price index for medical examinations, work days in the hospital, insurance premiums
Retail trade	–	Sales turnover	Price index for main categories of goods and services sold; consumer price index
	–	Gross profit margin for different categories of goods and services	Price index for different categories of goods and services sold
Banking services	–	Volume of sight and term deposits	Consumer price index; wholesale price index
	–	Number of checks cashed	Consumer price index or wholesale price index
	–	Net interests received	Index of purchasing power of gross receipts
Insurance	Insurance policy	Amounts insured: premiums paid	Volume index (number of premiums paid, etc.); general price indices (consumer or wholesale)

Air, rail, road, and sea transport	Passenger mile or ton mile	Number of passenger miles or ton miles transported; volume of freight; number of vehicles in circulation; fuel consumption	Index of wages paid. (In most cases the volume of output is calculated directly without reference to the price of the service rendered.)
Communications	Telephone conversation, telegram, letter, parcel	Number of telephone conversations, of telegrams, of letters, and of parcels	Consumer price index or wage index
Storage and dispatching	–	Volume or value of goods handled	Consumer price index
Public administration	–	Number of employees; number of hours worked	Index of wages paid; consumer price index
Education	–	Number of students or teachers; tuition paid	Wage and salary index, or consumer price index (in most cases the volume of output is calculated directly)
Domestic services	–	Number of employees	Consumer price index; wage index
Financial services, insurance, education; medical services, personal services, administration	–	N.B.: In many countries the production of these services as well as others is estimated on the basis either of employment in the sector concerned or of total wages paid, adjusted with a general or specific wage index	

1. Indications concerning the various methods used are mainly drawn from the following sources: V. R. Fuchs *The Service Economy*; V. R. Fuchs, ed. *Production and Productivity in the Service Industries*; Anthony D. Smith *The Measurement and Interpretation of Service Output Changes*; Irving Leveson *Productivity in Services, Issues for Analysis*; Derek W. Blades, Derek D. Johnston, Witold Marezewski *Service Activities in Developing Countries*, OECD, 1974. Examples in the table only give a very small sample of the variety of indicators used by national and international statistical services.

and not on the basis of the value embodied in the goods it helps to create. *In other words, the value of a service rests on the "lubricating" function which it plays in the various channels of economic activity.* In this, it differs fundamentally from any object created by man. At the same time, this particular function of services is a source of differentiation between the type of work performed by agents of the services sector and that performed by factory workers, craftsmen, and farm workers.

To illustrate the way in which services contribute to the valorization of goods, let us take the example of automobiles. Measured by the number of units produced, automobile output can be important, but the value of the product is nil if the only purpose it serves it to be lined up in thousands on huge factory storage lots. If the producer of automobiles does not pay or does not supply himself the advertising, transport, credit, and maintenance services necessary for the marketing of his carcasses of metal, these will remain objects without utility, inaccessible to the general public as long as they remain the private property of the manufacturer.

In different phases of the business cycle, some services such as advertising may play a more or less important role in the marketing of a given product and therefore in the determination of its final value. But in the long run, an ever-increasing proportion of the market value of goods consists of value-added in services which are incidental to manufacturing such as advertising, transport, labelling and packaging, credit, distribution, etc. *In final analysis, the development of service activities results in the transfer of value-added from the physical to the intangible product, from the concrete good to the abstract service act.*

The notion of service as an *act* of production calls for a definition of value which condemns the crippling notion of unproductive work inherited from Adam Smith [1960, ch. III, p. 314] and which makes it possible to depart from traditional methods of measurement based on the addition of physical quantities. Indeed, it is these methods which give the impression that the value-added per unit of factor employed in services is lower than it is in other sectors of economic activity. Their systematic bias comes from the fact that they do not take into account the valorization effect which services have on physical production in all types of economic systems, but especially in market economies where they play an important role in the search for sales outlets.

This complementary role results in the value produced in service activities being related to the value of the goods which they help to produce or sell in the sense that the efficiency of the service depends on its capacity to facilitate the manufacture or the distribution of the goods. In other words, services contribute a portion of *externality* to the value of physical production.

This portion of externality should be counted in the value of services, in addition to the direct cost of the factors employed in the corresponding activities.

The distribution of the value of services between these two components (externality and direct cost) varies with the degree of sophistication (quality) of services or their "cultural content" (see above). The externality portion becomes preponderant for services with a high scientific and technological content. Much more generally speaking, it can be said that in a given society the portion of externality of all services increases *pari passu* with the level of literacy and education of its population.[4]

The reference to the two components of the value of services makes it possible to look pragmatically at the problem of production in this sector, using as starting point the constituent elements of the value of goods in all economies where the separation between goods producing activities and services activities is not complete (which is still the case everywhere in the world at present). If one were to break down the value of a good, one would find that it contains a nonneligible proportion of services performed by individuals who work either within or outside the corresponding goods-manufacturing or -processing enterprises, in fields such as management, accounting, advertising, sales, etc. Similarly, the value of a good comprises the cost of transport effected on behalf of the enterprises either within the production area, for example, from the factory to the warehouse and vice versa, or outside it, for example, to the seaport or from the railway freight station to the warehouse and vice versa. The example of soya given in figure 3–1 is typical of the "trajectory" followed by a basic commodity from the place of cultivation or extraction to the final consumer. (The complexity of this trajectory increases considerably for more sophisticated goods.)

Since one part of the value-added by services originates inside the enterprise or the plant and another part outside, it is necessary for purposes of analysis to identify the reasons for the particular distribution between inside and outside services in each particular case. These reasons are numerous. Apart from economic factors, in particular the relative efficiency of producers of services working within goods producing enterprises compared to producers working independently outside them, there are also cultural and institutional factors which influence this distribution: certain traditions, whether or not confirmed by legislation, reserve certain services activities for independent producers. This is the case of most nonmarketable services such as defence, justice, police, etc., as well as of certain marketable services such as medicine.

The gains or losses of external economies arising from the fact that a given

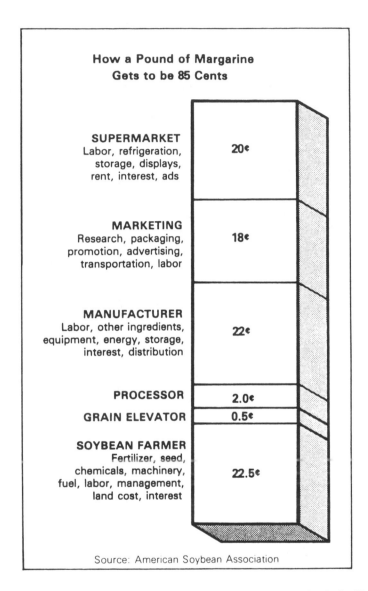

**How a Pound of Margarine
Gets to be 85 Cents**

SUPERMARKET
Labor, refrigeration,
storage, displays,
rent, interest, ads

20¢

MARKETING
Research, packaging,
promotion, advertising,
transportation, labor

18¢

MANUFACTURER
Labor, other ingredients,
equipment, energy, storage,
interest, distribution

22¢

PROCESSOR   2.0¢

GRAIN ELEVATOR   0.5¢

SOYBEAN FARMER
Fertilizer, seed,
chemicals, machinery,
fuel, labor, management,
land cost, interest

22.5¢

Source: American Soybean Association

Figure 3–1.   Components of the Retail Price of a Pound of Margarine in the United
States

activity is exercised inside or outside goods producing enterprises must also be evaluated in order to understand the effect of a given modification of the distribution between inside and outside activities on the contribution of services to the valorization of physical production. It is only once this particular element of value-added has been isolated that one can begin to address the problem of the productivity of service activities, either at the level of the enterprise or at the level of the economy as a whole.

If a service activity is transferred outside a goods producing enterprise the value added to the goods within this enterprise is reduced by two amounts: on one hand, an amount corresponding to the direct cost of the services in question and, on the other, an amount corresponding to the external economies produced by the service activity in question within the enterprise. If the services rendered outside the enterprise have the same direct cost and produce the same external economies, the final unit value of the goods in question will remain unchanged. On the other hand, if their direct cost is lower or if specialized services enterprises create more external economies for a given cost, the final unit value of the goods will be diminished by an equivalent amount, whereas the efficiency of the production-sales-consumption chain will be increased by the same amount. In other words, the total productivity of the economy will be increased.

The value added to final goods by services supplied *outside* goods producing enterprises is therefore composed of two elements: (1) *the transfer value*, which is equivalent to the value produced by services within the goods producing enterprise; (2) *the efficiency value*, which corresponds to the difference between the value produced by the same services depending on whether they are being supplied inside or outside the enterprise in question. In the case of services which are traditionally supplied by independent enterprises or individuals but which in the course of the economic development process are gradually absorbed within goods producing enterprises, it is clear that the definition of the transfer value must be reversed.

Each of the two components of the total value of services, i.e., the direct cost of factors and the external economies, enter into the transfer value and the efficiency value. The direct cost of factors is the only one of the two components which is known and measurable. It is therefore from this base that one must attempt to estimate the value of services output.

Let us take the hypothetical case of enterprise X which is entirely self-financed and which produces 1,000 tons of a good, with all services of design, engineering, market research, storage, sales, transport, etc., being integrated within this enterprise. Let us assume further that, while enterprise X continues to produce the same quantity of the same good, in the course of time it has gradually sold out its service activities which it now purchases from specialized independent firms. Although noneconomic reasons may be at the origin of such a transfer, normally it will be motivated by the fact that services purchased outside are cheaper than those produced from within the enterprise. Now, if the production and sales conditions remain the same for the goods producing enterprise X, it will continue to have recourse to the same services whatever their origin. In order to have an idea of the relative productivity of the services produced from outside the enterprise, we can therefore compare the direct cost of the factors employed in these activities to the direct cost of the factors employed for identical purposes within the enterprise *for a given quantity of goods* produced and sold by enterprise X. In heuristic notation, this can be expressed by the following equations:

$$V'_s = (C'_s + \frac{C_s}{C'_s}) B \qquad\qquad 3.1$$

$$B = \frac{1}{a}S \qquad\qquad 3.2$$

where V'_s = value-added (whether or not accounted for)[5] in service activities performed outside the enterprise
C_s and C'_s = direct cost of services supplied within and outside the enterprise, respectively;
B = quantity of goods produced;
S = services used for the production and sale of B;
$\frac{1}{a}$ = constant.

The expression $(C_s/C'_s)B$ represents additional external economies achieved after the transfer.

The assumption that there is a constant relationship between the volume of production of goods and the nature, number, or intensity of services utilized for the valorization of these goods allows a first approximation of the productivity of services, going beyond the simple ratio of turnover to factor cost.

On the other hand, it leaves unanswered two important questions.

First, it does not say whether there is a relationship between the quality of the services supplied and the number or intensity of service acts performed per unit of physical production. It can be assumed, however, that an increase in external economies is a sign of an increase in quality. There are then three possible outcomes: the final unit value of the goods is reduced (the economies realized in the form of an increase in quality without an increase in cost are passed on to consumers in the form of a lower price of the good); the final value remains unchanged but the quality of the goods increases; or the profits of the goods producing enterprise increase.

Second, the assumption of a constant ratio of services output to goods output, as well as the formula based on this assumption, leave completely unanswered the question of the *absolute* value of services output, since it excludes the possibility that V'_s may be greater than $(C'_s + C_s/C'_s)B$. In real life, it is quite possible that specialization in service activities may result in an increase of productivity greater than the difference between the direct cost of factors used by internalized, compared with externalized, services.[6] In order to know this, however, one needs to have a precise idea of what a unit of service is, a condition which is far from being easily fulfilled in all cases (see next section).

Another problem concerns the distribution between factor costs and external economies before and after the transfer of service activities outside the firm. It has often been noted that average earnings in independent service activities are higher than in industry although the average level of qualification of the factors is lower in services. One possible explanation is that a portion of the invoiced value of additional external economies realized by these enterprises is passed through to the salaries of their staff. It is also possible that the development of independent service activities in the competitive setting of a market economy brings about an increase in the scientific, technical, and cultural content of the services supplied as a result of the need to better respond to the demand of user enterprises i.e., those which have turned to the market rather than continuing to supply the same services within their own organization. In the latter case, it can be expected that the value e'_s (see note 6) will increase out of all proportion with the increase in external economies resulting from the transfer of service activities outside the physical production sector.[7]

Definition of a Unit of Service

It is in this area that any study of services faces its greatest challenge both theoretically and practically. The difficulty has to be faced, however, if there is any hope of ever answering the question of whether the productivity of services is higher on average when these services are independent economic activities than when they are integrated to the goods producing sector. In turn, the answer to this question will provide guidance to answer another, equally important, question, which is whether modern economies characterized by a strong concentration of production in the services sector are condemned to secular decline compared with societies which are still in the phase of industrialization.

The difficulty to be faced was identified more than 20 years ago by McMahon and Worswick [1961], in the following terms:

> Take the policeman. One would be hard put to it to "quantify" his output. (Ultimately it might be something like the number of crimes which did not occur in relation to the number that did—but such statistics are hard to come by.) But one cannot here fall back satisfactorily on our second measure either: we do not pay him by results. His timely presence may save the Crown jewels one week, while in the next he may be called on for nothing more than an explanation of how to get to Westminster Abbey. His pay packet each week is the same. That, indeed, is all the money we ever pay him. Hence it is on this that the statistician must seize to value his output.
>
> The same applies to almost all government officials, members of the armed forces, parsons, and others. It is the best that can be done, no doubt, but of course it utterly prohibits the unfortunate policeman or parson from ever increasing his productivity unless he gets a raise.

The policeman, the fireman, the guard, the receptionist, the churchman, the state in its functions of maintaining law and order, of protecting property and individuals, of justice, etc., give rise to the greatest difficulty when it comes to evaluating not only the total value but also the unit value of the services they perform.

These activities are a good illustration of the characteristics of *variability*, *discontinuity*, and *externality* of services: changes of intensity and quality depending on the circumstances; discontinuity in time and space; indirect effects on the market value and the intrinsic value of goods. These characteristics are such that there are probably no two services which are identical, in the sense of goods being identical, so that the notion of unit of service is somewhat of a fiction as is the notion of single market price for services since, at best, services can be comparable or similar. How, indeed, can one fix a price for the presence of a guard when his supply of services varies in nature and intensity from day to day and from hour to hour?

Having said this, it is appropriate to recall that there is also an element of distortion of reality in the conventional definition of units of physical goods. Every notion of unity is based on general principles of measurement such as weight, dimension, or volume, which are applied to particular objects without taking into account, or only by the way, the quality of the object being measured. "A rose is a rose," said Gertrude Stein. This is approximately true of many goods whose technical specifications are so simple that they may be considered "standard" goods: for example, a tennis ball, a loaf of bread, a pair of nylon stockings, etc. Differentiation of products, monopolistic competition, and intra-industrial specialization do exist, but in final analysis there is no great difficulty in admitting that physical goods can be classified in a relatively small number of categories, irrespective of quality differences within each category: for example, color television sets with a 26-inch or a 12-inch screen, automobiles with different engine sizes, unpainted or varnished wooden furniture, suitcases made of leather or of plastic materials, etc.

The same sort of approach can be followed for services. First, it is necessary to identify indicators of performance which are adapted to the nature of service acts being performed, such as time, intensity, distance travelled, availability, speed, etc. Second, it is necessary to identify operational concepts related to these performance indicators and which make it possible more or less arbitrarily to mark off *bundles of service acts* representing units of services, by analogy with the categories of products mentioned previously: for example, an hour of screenplay, a mile of transportation, a day of gardening, a round of guard duty, a piano lesson, a bus journey. Finally, and this is specific to services, it is necessary to relate the number of units of services produced and their cost to the physical production (individual, sectoral, or national) whose final value they contribute in fixing, taking into account the reasoning followed in the first part of the present chapter.

In themselves the performance indicators are fairly easy to define, since they are as intangible as the services which they help to measure: time, speed, availability, etc., as indicated above. The only problem is to choose indicators that give a fairly good idea of the productivity of the factors employed in a given service activity. For example, to evaluate a transport service one has a choice between the following main criteria of quality: speed, time, security, regularity, availability, flexibility, possibility to ensure door-to-door delivery, comfort. On the other hand, the operational concepts used to identify bundles of service acts require a more thorough analysis of the nature of the particular services to which they apply, because their role is essentially that of conventional measurements taking the place of the concrete data used to identify physical goods.

We have seen earlier (table 3–1) the various types of indicators used by statisticians to estimate the total value of output of services by sector or by enterprise. In certain cases, these indicators make use of the concept of unit of output (number of checks cashed, number of passenger miles, etc.), but generally speaking they merely show the turnover of the sector or of the enterprise concerned. It is therefore nor possible to deduct real or nominal costs per unit of output from such indicators nor, consequently, the productivity of factors employed. For the moment, we shall limit ourselves to noting these deficiencies, but it is clear that much research will need to be carried out in order to improve existing statistical methods.

Characteristics of Nonmarket Services[8]

A number of collective services present the peculiarity that from the moment they are produced they can be supplied to an indeterminate number of consumers without any increase in cost; such is the case for television programs. Nonmarket services are collective services which it is more economical to supply outside the market than on a commercial basis, or which it is technically impossible to market because the nature of the service supplied to the individual consumer is not defined clearly enough. Examples of such services are police services, national defense, space exploration, diplomatic services, etc. [see Shoup, 1969, p. 67; also Commentary to chapter 5].

The difficulties inherent in the estimation of the value of output of services are much greater for nonmarketable than for other services. Generally speaking, the output of these services cannot be estimated either on the basis of their supply (number of units produced) nor on the basis of the demand for them (number of units consumed or number of consumers)—not to speak of the fact that the choice of an indicator of unit output is fraught with particular uncertainty because the very application of the notion of product to such services is questionable. In addition, it is not possible to base an estimation on the total value of output (turnover) because there are no money flows corresponding to the supply of such services. It is for this reason that in practice, statisticians estimate the value of production of government services or services supplied by public entities, on the sole basis of the cost of factors employed.

This situation is interesting in two respects. First, due to the growing influence of government in the economy of most countries, and therefore to the growing role of public services in total output, the evaluation of gross national product (GNP) becomes more and more problematical. Such uncertainty surrounding the evaluation of GNP adds to the difficulties resulting from the increase in the share of marketable services in total output. Secondly, since there is no market for nonmarketable services, these services do not have a price and even less a "market price," that is, a unique price corresponding to well-defined service acts. This is a special feature of a general characteristic of services, namely, that an important part of their contribution to total welfare takes the form of external economies and in this regard, each service act has its own value which depends as much on its quality as on its utility for the user. Under these conditions, the notion of marginal utility as a basis for the determination of market price becomes somewhat blurred. In this regard nonmarket services represent extreme cases which serve to underline the fundamental differences between the services economy and the goods economy.[9]

It is interesting to note that in practice, suppliers of public or private collective services seek as much as possible to free themselves from the technical constraints of this type of service by referring to "standards" or to "minimums" of performance more or less arbitrarily chosen. The service acts defined in those terms are supposed to produce more or less constant results, which makes them seem almost like physical goods. This likeness is sometimes stressed by the use of trademarks, advertising slogans, decorative elements, or by dressing up service personnel in uniforms. The whole of the franchising industry is based on this approach. In certain cases the standardization of the service product even makes it possible to commercialize services which are generally considered as nonmarketable. Typical examples of this are private police and protection services, although their distribution is somewhat limited due to the fact that they necessarily cater to homogeneous groups of people, each member of which attaches the same value to them and is therefore prepared to pay the same price for them.

In the area of industrial standardization, the problems of mutual recognition of test results and of accreditation of testing laboratories relate to the definition of harmonized testing methods and procedures, whose function is to guarantee the quality and the regularity of the service acts which the tests themselves represent. As this activity is both scientific and technical in nature, it represents a kind of service that is all but elementary, and it is therefore not surprising if progress in harmonization is slow.

Notes

1. On the evaluation of the value produced in services, see *inter alia* McMahon and Worswick [1961] and Anthony D. Smith [1972, pp. 109–114].

2. Authors who have given thought to this question in less macroeconomic terms than their colleagues include Shoup [1969], McMahon and Worswick [1961], Hall [1968], Gustafsson [1979], and Tucker [1979].

3. The French for service act, service performed or rendered, or benefits obtained from a service, is *prestation*. In the absence of a similar word in English, *prestation* has previously been translated as *service act*. As used here, the word *act* refers more to a general characteristic of service functions than to individual benefits or effects produced by services.

4. This reasoning, if stretched to its logical limit, would lead to the conclusion that in advanced economies, where the role of service activities in national production is predominant, external economies represent a preponderant portion of the total product of human activity. Given the fact that external economies are not included in national accounting, the national product of advanced countries would be underestimated accordingly. This would also be true for other countries, but the phenomenon would be much less marked in the latter because they are technically and scientifically less developed.

5. In the case of C_s [greater than] C'_s, V'_s [is greater than] V_s, that is, the final value of goods produced is higher when services are externalized. However, as the difference consists in

external economies, the supplemental value obtained is not accounted for. It can be assimilated (see below) to an increase in the quality of the good produced.

6. It will be noted that equations 3.1 and 3.2 do not take into account the external economies which represent an equivalent share of the transfer value and of the efficiency value, so that the implicit expression for the transfer value is $V_s = C_s$ instead of $V_s = C_s + e_s$, where e represents the external economies in question. An increase in production more than proportional to the difference between direct costs would imply that e'_s is greater than e_s.

7. The reasoning that precedes applies both to externalization and internalization of services. It is recalled that externalization is used here only as an example.

8. The economic nature of services covered by the notion of "public goods" is analyzed in great depth by Carl S. Shoup [1969, ch 4]. On this question, see also A. R. Prest [1982].

9. The following quotation is interesting from this point of view: "Information can be acquired by expanding resources but, once one has it, it is not diminished if someone else has it as well. It is an example of a public good. For quite obvious reasons the Fundamental Welfare Theorems cannot hold when there are public goods. Indeed, the market economy will perform disastrously in such cases. No one will invest in the production of information if its market price is necessarily zero. That is why we have patent and copyright laws." [Hahn, 1982]

4 THE FUTURE OF SERVICES SOCIETIES AND OF ECONOMIC POLICY

Without its being necessary at this stage to examine in depth the question of the contribution of services to economic welfare, their importance in developed as well as developing economies is sufficiently documented to invite questions on the influence which their expansion can exert on the social evolution and on the economic policies of the postindustrial era.

To begin with, one major issue to be addressed is whether service activities must be seen as choking the growth of advanced economies or, on the contrary, as opening new avenues of development beyond the present industrial framework. The problem has two aspects: that of quantitative growth, and that of qualitative development allowing the competitiveness of the economies concerned to be maintained or to improve with or without a concurrent increase in physical well-being. There are also two dimensions to the problem: national and international. At the national level, the internal competitiveness of economies determines their capacity to evolve toward new modes of production and to adapt their productive and social structures to these new modes. At the international level, their external competitiveness determines the capacity of economies to preserve favorable terms of trade vis-à-vis countries which supply goods or services essential to their upkeep and development.

Modification of Production Structures and the Crisis of Industrial Societies: Are Services To Blame?

Many of the greatest economists of the nineteenth century were concerned with the long-term prospects for growth based on the continuous accumulation of industrial capital. The lowering of the rate of return linked to this accumulation led some of them to conclude to the advent of a stationary state in which economic activity would only allow for the simple renewal of productive capacities [see, for example, Mill, 1965, ch. VI]. Other interpretations were given of the probable evolution of capitalism. Marxist economists questioned the theory of profit as the engine of growth. They saw it acting as a brake on consumption, hence as a major cause of more and more frequent and severe crises of overproduction, which would spell the doom of the system in the not-too-distant future. More recently, the rigidities introduced in the system by social legislation adopted in periods of economic expansion, and on which it is not possible to backtrack in periods of crisis, have been presented by liberal economists as the cause of a long-term slowdown in growth which could lead to total paralysis and decline. For their part, Keynesian economists have seen direct intervention of governments in the development of main economic aggregates (saving, consumption, investment) as a means of overcoming the rigidities of the system in periods of crisis, hence of avoiding the deflationary spirals announced by others.

Nowadays, the future of capitalism does not seem to preoccupy Western economists as much as previously. Some of them have acquired an unshakable faith in continuous economic growth and in the technical progress which underlies it. Others, fascinated by the triumph of industrialism and the joys of consumerism, are a long way from sharing the humanistic concerns of those Victorian gentlemen who were the founding fathers of modern economics [see, for example, Mill, 1962]. In addition, after the Second World War and until the end of the 1960s, hardly a political leader ever expressed any concern about what the extraordinary explosion of material satisfaction which the whole Western world derived from an apparently unlimited economic expansion held in store for the future.

However, the economic crisis which began in the early 1970s has given rise to new preoccupations concerning the future of industrial societies, by showing them to be vulnerable not only to their own contradictions but also to external pressures. Different schools of thought have emerged as a result, which have in common a normative analysis of the crisis but propose different solution. For the followers of the Club of Rome, the race toward physical expansion is the cause of a net reduction in welfare, notably as a result of the accelerated depletion of the nonrenewable resources of the planet and of the destruction of the "ecosystem."[1] Another school of thought, to which Alain Barrère[2] and J. K. Galbraith[3] appear to belong, attributes the inflation and unemployment whose simultaneous increases have disorganized Western economies in the 1970s, to the process of accumulation of capital, to the relationship between accumulation and rate of return, and to productive and associative structures put in place during 30 years of almost uninterrupted growth. These authors search for ways of fostering stable and lasting development, both quantitative and qualitative, through new forms of investment and new modes of distribution of value-added (including, for Alain Barrère, job-sharing).

A third school of thought is composed of theoricians of a "new" or "self-centered" development, to which belong François Perroux[4] as well as certain authors originating from the Third World[5] or defending Third World viewpoints.[6] Some of the concerns of these authors are similar to the anti-materialist approach of the ecologists or to the anti-determinism of an Alan Barrère or a J. K. Galbraith.

In general, studies of the future prospects of capitalism pay little attention to service activities. This is due to the macroeconomic approach they follow and to the fact that they stress the fundamental mechanisms of the system as such (accumulation, profit, income distribution, etc.) rather than sectoral problems. Such studies are nonetheless interesting due to the very fact that they pay little attention to services. They implicitly consider services as being subject to the same constraints and to the same forces of the market as goods, unless they simply consider, as did Adam Smith, that they do not belong to the category of productive activities. Until now, the assumption that the production and sale of services and goods take place under similar conditions has never been seriously questioned. This can hardly be held against the economists of the nineteenth century, for whom industry was the thing of the future, but in our century where economic activity is turning more and more toward services, it is surprising that so few researchers should have followed the trail opened by Colin Clark in 1957.[7]

Since services are not directly accused of causing the slowdown in growth or the inflation and unemployment which seem to mark a turning point in the evolution of capitalist economies, one could conclude that they have little to do with these phenomena. However, certain observations would seem to point to the contrary.[8]

Available statistics show that average productivity is lower in the sector of services than in either industry or agriculture. Given that there is a long-term tendency for the share of services in total output to increase, the slowdown in growth appears to be inevitable. Moreover, since the apparent productivity of services is lower, the average rate of inflation should be higher for a

their combination, telematics, has revolutionized the relationship between embodied and disembodied services in the majority of human production and consumption activities. First, it has made it possible to overcome one of the main obstacles to the development of services activities, namely the distance between service provider and service user.[9] Second, it has facilitated the application of technical know-how in goods production, notably through automation, robotics, and remote control not only of manufacturing but also of storage, accounting, and management. Finally, it has made possible the embodiment in goods of elements of information and data processing techniques which improve their performance (that is, the services provided by them). A typical example is the introduction of computers on board transport equipment.

The introduction and development of these new techniques modifies production methods in two essential ways: by reducing the use of labor on the shop floor, and by reducing the real time necessary for the execution of the designing, planning, engineering, managing, innovating, surveillance, and monitoring tasks, all of which determine the scope and rapidity of technical progress, hence the rate of increase of material well-being in any society.

It may be noted in passing that the sophisticated equipment used in telecommunication and data processing is itself a carrier of advanced industrial technology whose design and development stimulates investment and absorbs, at least in part, the labor displaced by services activities using such equipment. This phenomenon is similar to the absorption by industry of factors of production which it had itself made superfluous in handicraft and agriculture.

Opposite to these developments, there is a rapid increase in the demand for consumption services, linked to sports and tourism, audiovisual products, home computing, etc. This demand orients the production of services toward activities with a relatively low cultural content and which have little accelerating effect on the development of knowledge, in contrast to the effect of the demand for goods on technical progress. What is the reason for this difference of impact? It is difficult to find an answer to this question because the role of services consumption in the development of knowledge is not fully understood, and it may well be that the difference is more apparent than real. It remains true, in any case, that the conditions of production of goods, and particularly the possibility to reap economies of scale, are such that an increase in final demand for goods stimulates the search for technical means of lowering unit cost of production. On the contrary, an increase in demand for consumption services tends to lead to the multiplication of agents supplying these services and to the proliferation of points of sale, neither of which result in more than marginal reductions of unit costs or in any improvement in the quality of services. It is perhaps true, therefore, that services are more effective carriers of cultural development when they contribute to physical production, which is the most elaborate form of domination of nature by man.

In practice, the weak accelerator effect of demand for consumption services, if it is confirmed by analysis and experience,[10] will affect the development of advanced economies in the postindustrial era. The question of whether the expansion of the share of service activities in total output leads economies into a dead-end from the growth point of view or if, on the contrary, it constitutes a chance of regaining the dynamism which they have presently lost, will depend on whether consumption services become relatively more important than services linked to the improvement of production methods both in the industrial and in the nonphysical sector. This is true both for services supplied by the private sector in response to financially solvent demand by final consumers or intermediate users, and for nonmarketable services supplied by public authorities and by the various organizations and enterprises that depend on them.

In any event, Smithian prejudices vis-à-vis services in general are not a good remedy to the growth crisis of Western economies. The essence of all value-added is knowledge, and such knowledge is contained in a great number of services considered as unproductive by the classics, including artistic work. Economic policy must therefore not seek to slow down the expansion of services, but on the contrary to orient it toward areas or branches where services can perform their valorization function most effectively. In addition, investment on a large scale in education, training, research, and communication is indispensable in a society where *every* productive activity has an ever-increasing cultural content.

Indeed, the fact that in the actual phase of transformation of the conditions of production, software becomes more important than hardware as a factor in the expansion of industry and advanced services (telecommunications, computer, and financial services) means that in many cases concerns over the "preservation of the industrial base" hark back to the outdated concepts of the industrial revolution, when mechanization was the principal engine of expansion. The traditional machine now gives way to the robot, and the robot itself gives way to more sophisticated types of thinking tools. For more than 10 years, sales of software by major multinational enterprises in the computer sector have grown by 30 to 40 percent per year, compared with 10 percent for hardware.

Services and International Competitiveness

What is true of national economies also holds for international trade. This consists more and more in the interchange of knowledge, either directly in the form of cross-border flows of services or indirectly in the form of trade in goods with a high technological content. The technology elaborated by goods producing enterprises is also more and more a subject of trade per se, as equipment compatible with this technology is increasingly manufactured under licence in software-importing countries. Nevertheless, a presence on foreign markets remains indispensable for most firms exporting services in order to adapt their supply to the specific needs of users, as discussed above. Consequently, apart from telecommunications and computer services, only a small number of services are traded at a distance, that is, without the direct intervention of an agent of the service producer in the importing market.

This being said, it is a fact that services represent a growing share of international trade either in the form of cross-border transactions or of services provided by enterprises established on foreign markets and whose repatriated profits are recorded as credits in the balance of payments. Commercial policy must take this fact into account more and more. In particular, attention must be paid to the transfers of resources that result from positive or negative net financial flows related to services which are classified as "invisibles" or concealed under the item "capital movements" of the balance of payments.

However, neither economic theory nor international economic diplomacy as currently practiced have prepared governments to face up to the entirely new problems posed by the ultra-rapid development of trade in services. The rules of conduct which major trading countries have committed themselves to follow were designed for trade in goods, leaving aside all movements of capital or factors which substitute in one way or another for this trade. Since a large number of services sold abroad are supplied by branches, subsidiaries, or representative offices, the restraints imposed by governments on the activities of these firms are not subject to any agreed international trade disciplines. As a result, the legal vacuum in which trade in services takes place leaves the door wide open to all sorts of restrictive actions aimed at checking or reducing competition in this sector.

In the field of trade in goods, the theory of comparative advantage offers a good basis for evaluating the relative efficiency with which a given economic entity uses the factors with which it is endowed. This theory implies that in each economic entity, goods are produced with a combination of factors that reflects the factor endowments of the entity in question. Thus, goods which can be produced with a relatively high proportion of labor to capital tend to be manufactured, according to the theory, in countries where labor is relatively abundant, whereas goods whose production requires a high proportion of capital tend to be manufactured where capital is abundant. Consequently, when a firm invests abroad, it generally does so to manufacture goods with the combination of factors which corresponds to the endowment of the country or countries where the investment takes place.

The situation is quite different for services. Since the essence of a service is the quality of the service act, it is the capacity to ensure this quality which determines the greater or lesser competitiveness of service enterprises on foreign markets. Now, in order to ensure this quality, the service enterprise that establishes abroad uses either imported production factors or, at least, a combination of factors identical to that of the home country and *not* of the host country. This raises the question of the meaning of comparative advantage in the field of services. Does it consist in possessing transferable production capacities which have nothing to do with the factor endowments of the economic entities where the production takes place? If so, it is more relevant to speak of absolute or intrinsic advantage than of comparative advantage. In this case, however, international competitiveness ceases to bear much relation to the famous factor endowments.

Moreover, considering that most of the capital utilized in services is human capital (knowledge and experience), it is hard to see what role the ratio of physical capital to labor can play in determining the competitiveness of economies to produce such and such types of services. While it is true that services employ very sophisticated machines such as computers, the comparative advantage in producing such machines should not be confused with the competitiveness in supplying the services of which they are the vehicle. Scientists of the Third World are no less able than those of industrialized countries, and their only drawback is a more limited access to technical means of measurement and computing compared to the latter. It is probably true that *accumulated* human capital is an important factor in the production of sophisticated machines, but this is a perfectly normal feature of every industrial activity, and it cannot be logically deduced from it that the classical theory of comparative advantage applies to services *as such*.

International competitiveness is measured by positive and negative flows in the balance of payments of trading nations. In the case of goods, the merchandise account is a key indicator of the competitiveness of a country. On the other hand, competitiveness in the field of services is not necessarily reflected in the "invisibles" item of the current balance.

Only services that are the subject of direct international transactions are included in this item, plus the returns on foreign investment and interest payments or receipts on loaned capital. (For a more detailed description of this item, see the next chapter.) The services supplied by branches, subsidiaries, or representative offices abroad are not included in the balance-of-payments accounts. The latter only record profits of the enterprises concerned which are repatriated in their home country. There is, of course, no fixed proportion between repatriated profits and services sold, and in any event, repatriated profits only account for a small share of the turnover of foreign establishments. Moreover, balance-of-payments statistics include in the same item the profits repatriated by branches, etc., of goods producing enterprises and services producing enterprises. Under these conditions, it is difficult to use any particular flow of payments as an indicator of the competitive position of an economy in the field of services.

It should be noted that this difficulty is common to services and to goods insofar as repatriated profits of foreign investments do not permit a precise evaluation of the efficiency of the capital factor in foreign undertakings. For services, however, the situation is somewhat different in the sense that this difficulty extends in most cases to all or most of the factors of production employed abroad, since service enterprises use staff from the home country in order to ensure a quality of service equal to that provided by the main office, and on which they have built their commercial success and their reputation in the home country.

But the problem is not just statistical. Competitiveness in services depends on the contribution of services activities performed in host countries on the overall economic activity of the latter. This contribution can be measured according to the method suggested in chapter 3. The economic impact of services sold abroad depends on the manner in which they adapt to the productive and commercial structures specific to foreign markets, that is, on the amount of external economies they contribute to the functioning of the economies concerned. If they are well adapted to the needs of foreign markets, they can play an important role in the total trade of the service-exporting countries concerned. It is not simply the fact of being able to produce efficient services better than others and at lower-cost (which in the field of goods would mean that they have a comparative advantage) which makes it possible for enterprises in that position to establish themselves successfully on all markets. Thus, certain computer hardware and software producing firms which are very successful commercially on the markets of developed countries are sometimes incapable of penetrating less-developed markets because their modern methods are not adapted to the needs of these markets.

Finally, the particular features of international trade in services throw a different light on the question of transfer of resources compared to the treatment of this issue in the field of goods. Generally speaking, when transactions consist in a movement of factors of production toward "importing" countries, this results in an initial transfer of resources toward these countries. This transfer is only compensated after a certain time has elapsed by the repatriation of the profits of exporting enterprises[11] established abroad or, in the short run, by reverse flows of investment from foreign enterprises into the exporting country concerned. On the other hand, when the transactions consist of direct sales from the exporting country to importing countries through a means of transport, which in the case of services can be a means of telecommunications, the transfer of resources depends solely on the evolution of the terms of trade: net transfers are positive if the terms of trade are favorable and negative if they are unfavorable to the exporting country.

Now, it so happens that in trade in goods, since there is no need to produce at the point of sale, transfers of resources (positive or negative) are in most cases effected through the terms of trade, whereas on the contrary in the case of services they are in most cases effected through investment.

This difference of nature between goods and services calls for certain revisions of the theory of international trade, as well as of the trade policies of service-exporting countries and of the principles governing them.

Gaps in the Theory of International Trade

The theory of international trade as we know it was elaborated in terms of the *industrial* mode of production. It applies to goods which can be manufactured in large quantities thanks to the use of machines. The uniformity of the product and the automatization of manufacturing tasks make it possible to reach economies of scale so long as entrepreneurs have access to sufficiently large markets. Competition takes place through the product itself. The fact that the specifications of this product vary little from one producer to another facilitates the establishment of a single market price for the product. The theory of international trade therefore bases itself on the assumption of free competition allowing for the formation of a unique or single price at the world level for each product. As we have seen above, in the case of services, the single price is the exception rather than the rule. The mechanistic vision of the market therefore no longer has much relevance for understanding the phenomenon of trade in services.

The dominant theory of international trade concludes to the economic efficiency of free trade. It implies a priori the adoption of liberal trade policies by governments that espouse the theory. Such a foregone conclusion becomes questionable as soon as it ceases to be possible to mechanically extend the theory of trade in goods to trade in services. In fact, several factors militate in favor of a less clear-cut approach.

First, the fact that many services are the source of externalities, in particular nonmarketable services and those which have the character of public utilities, such as transport and telecommunications, introduces a disparity between their cost of production and their price which makes them ideal candidates for the intervention of governments in the market. Whatever the economic efficiency of the methods used by governments to provide those services and the moral justification for their intervention, which is to ensure an equitable supply of the services in question to all classes of consumers, state enterprises and state monopolies cannot be expected to behave according to free-trade principles in the sectors of activity concerned.

The need to invest and to establish abroad in order to supply certain services is another reason to think that free trade is not necessarily the answer to the preoccupations of governments in this area. To begin with, we are essentially dealing here with movements of factors and not trade. The theory of trade remains practically silent on movements of factors except to recognize that these can be a substitute for trade in goods and vice versa. But the establishment of enterprises, often accompanied by their own manpower, on foreign territories is not without creating difficulties of integration of a sociocultural nature, which lead host governments to intervene by regulating the right of establishment. Operational principles derived from the theory of free trade as it applies to goods, such as the most-favored nation principle and the national treatment principle, are not necessarily applicable without change to trade in services taking place through branches, subsidiaries, or representative offices of foreign enterprises.

Since services which are internationally traded have a high cultural content, they carry with them not only knowledge but also mental attitudes, working habits, and life styles. It is for this reason that governments have a tendency to regulate with great care not only the establishment of foreign service enterprises but also international transactions in services generally.

Thus, the creation of data banks and the transborder processing of data through telecomputing facilities have given rise in many countries to reactions in favor of the protection of the privacy of individuals and of intellectual property.[12]

It should be noted, however, that the attitudes of governments toward the problem of preserving cultural heritage differ markedly depending on the extent to which they are convinced of the superiority of the liberal economic model. In most countries with an ancient civilization, capitalism has been superimposed on previous political and ideological structures which have left more or less visible marks on life styles and mental attitudes, and which continue to form an important part of the cultural heritage [see Amin, 1973, ch. 1]. The governments of the countries concerned take these factors into account in deciding on any particular course of action. Conversely, some nations were born just at the time when capitalism was beginning to take hold, while others did not have a sufficiently strong cultural tradition to resist the influence of the "economism" which, according to Samir Amin [1973, p. 20], is "the true religion of capitalist societies." The governments of these two latter types of countries, insofar as they follow the lead of the free marketeers, are more prone to conceive of any economic activity as a means of making profit. Consequently, they attach little importance to the problems of sociocultural integration which are seen as a constraint by countries in the previous category.

International Economic Cooperation Revisited

International trade in goods is governed by a more or less coherent set of rules of behavior to which governments subscribe, either multilaterally or in the framework of bilateral or regional agreements, or, still, by virtue of international common law. Save in exceptional cases, the same does not hold for services. Certain bilateral trade treaties deal with service activities, but they hardly go beyond commitments of a general character relating to nondiscrimination with respect to the right of establishment and partial or full national treatment. There are also a number of multilateral agreements managed by intergovernmental organizations such as the International Civil Aviation Organization (ICAO) and the International Maritime Organization (IMO), both being specialized agencies of the United Nations, but their mandate in the trade field is limited and their activities are essentially technical in character. The Organization for Economic Cooperation and Development (OECD) has adopted two codes of conduct, one on the liberalization of invisible transactions and the other on the liberalization of capital movements, but the provisions of these codes are not really binding,[13] and they are partly made inoperative as a result of the reservations maintained by signatory governments to their application. Consequently, for all practical purposes international service activities take place in a legal vacuum.

This situation has many advantages but also some drawbacks. The absence of rules facilitates the expansion of the international activities of dynamic enterprises in high-technology sectors, where freedom of action compensates for the considerable financial risks involved. Similarly, in traditional sectors such as maritime transport it stimulates innovation in the organization of transactions as well as the lowering of production costs: for example, through recourse to flags of convenience. The disadvantage of the lack of intergovernmental cooperation in the field of services is that governments are free to impose any kind of restriction on the activities of foreign service enterprises on their territory. Apart from the fact that all kinds of measures are allowed, governments are not inhibited by any contractual commitment which would constrain them to offer compensation to their trading partners for restrictive measures taken against the latter's enterprises. The lack of transparency and predictability of their policies in this regard create a climate of uncertainty which is not favorable to the development of trade on the basis of confidence and long-term planning. The predatory behavior of which multinational service enterprises are sometimes accused can partly be explained by the search for short-term profits as a means of hedging against the uncertainty created by the unpredictable character of the policies of host countries.

The well-known fact that economists and governments have only recently begun to take an interest in the role of services in the economy is one of the reasons why services have been neglected in most agreements governing international trade. Another reason is that economists and governments alike have always believed that service activities are essentially confined to the internal market, so that governmental measures affecting the exercise of these activities were not considered as negotiable at the international level. Nowadays, new techniques facilitating the exchange of services have brought to the attention of some governments the importance of these activities to the trade of their countries with the rest of the world, while others continue to see them as a means rather than an end. Whereas the former now wish to submit services to the forces of international competition, the latter are concerned with maintaining a large degree of autonomy in the development of this sector in their own countries.

The gradual liberalization of trade in goods during the last three decades has reinforced economic integration among the countries which have participated in it. In the days when markets were more or less closed, the main barriers to trade were restrictive measures applied at the border. These were therefore the first target of liberalization efforts. The progress made in reducing such barriers has brought to light other types of barriers which take the form of regulations applicable in the domestic markets of the countries concerned. The restrictive effect of such measures was, in most cases, due to their disparity, their complexity, and to the nontransparent manner in which they were applied. In order for the process of trade liberalization to move forward, it was therefore necessary to turn attention to this type of measure with a view to harmonizing and simplifying them and making their application more transparent. As a result of these efforts, the economic integration of the participating countries was further strengthened. The liberalization of trade in services, in particular if it covered the activities of branches or subsidiaries of foreign enterprises, could be construed as a third step along the road to integration. The question is, which countries are ready to take this step and within what time frame?

It is still too early to reply. Presumably, countries which have not made much progress in the liberalization of their trade will want to proceed step-by-step with the integration of their economies in the world economy. Consequently, they will not be in a hurry to enter into negotiations aiming at liberalization of trade in services, especially if this should lead to subjecting their domestic regulations in the fields of investment and right of establishment to international disciplines. The liberalization of trade in services at world level can nevertheless be beneficial for these countries even if they do not participate directly in the exercise. The establishment of a competitive climate in this area would in the long run be beneficial for their exports in the fields where they are competitive which, however, presupposes that the protection of their internal market will be put to good avail to develop their productive capacities.

In any international negotiation, the scope of the results achieved by any government depends on the reciprocity that it grants to its partners. Such reciprocity is not necessarily absolute, and, in fact, the practical effect of the contractual commitment made is not always measurable. Moreover, the circumstances which prevent a country from making a liberalization effort comparable to that of its partners are taken into account when such consideration is in the collective interest of all the participants in the negotiation. Hence, the fact of participating, albeit as a spectator, in a joint liberalization enterprise, and thereby to support it, can be a gesture of considerable political significance for those governments that pursue the enterprise with a view to achieving concrete results.

If there were to be agreement to deal with the problems of services at the international level, solutions could conceivably be found along the lines of existing agreements on the limitation of the restrictive effects of national regulations in the field of goods. The negotiated arrangements could address specific measures such as subsidies or mandatory standards or deal with problems on a sectoral basis covering, for example, banking, insurance, maritime transport, etc. In the latter case they would deal with all types of measures applicable in each of these sectors. The broader the agenda of a multilateral trade negotiation, the greater are its chances of success.

Postindustrial Economic and Social Policies

In the field of national economic management, it may be necessary to invent new decisional and consultative structures which take into account the growing importance of services as sources of cultural and technological development. The first step might consist in making more room for service enterprises in national economic consultation mechanisms. At the same time, the organization of service work requires more intensive consultations of all productive agents in service enterprises than it does in industry.

Structural adjustment policies should, from now on, give priority to all those service activities which constitute the most advanced forms of production in society, such as scientific research, education, training, and the arts. This preference for activities with a high intellectual content should help to consolidate the maturity of the economies of industrially advanced countries. This would probably entail both a somewhat smaller volume growth of goods production and a more systematic pursuit of quality improvements in all fields, including that of goods.

In relation to demand management policy, in particular fiscal policy, the development of a new sector of activity which has so far been largely neglected implies a fundamental change in the mechanisms of adjustment to variations in final demand. The greater stability of demand for services should lead to a tempering of reflationary policies and a hardening of deflationary policies. With cyclical fluctuations being naturally less pronounced in postindustrial economies, the risk of inflationary pressures getting out of control will be greater than in the past in periods of economic recovery, whereas demand-dampening measures will have less of a deflationary effect. This asymmetry is due to a stronger income effect in favor of services in the first case, and a stronger substitution effect in their favor in the second. As a result, the "tangible" production sectors draw little benefit from the upswing and bear the full brunt of the downswing in economic activity.

Finally, the fact that services production is by nature less collective than industrial production should normally lead to the gradual loss of influence of trade unions, whose cohesiveness rests on the monotony of work and whose pugnacity draws its strength from a common indifference toward the goals of their enterprises. In line with this development, social security measures could be better adapted to the circumstances of each individual as they reflect his/her contribution to the qualitative development of society.

Notes

1. This approach is developed in *Limits to Growth* and in the writings of A. Peccei [1981] and O. Giarini [1980].

2. See *La crise n'est pas ce que l'on croit* [Barrère, 1981].

3. See, for example, his recent article in the *Harvard Business Review* [1982].

4. See his recent book *Pour une philosophie du nouveau développement* [1981].

5. For example, Samir Amin [1973] and M. Elmandjara.

6. For example, those connected with the Society for International Development, a private organization devoted to supporting the Third World.

7. Colin Clark was the first to dientify services as a distinct sector of activity in the *Conditions of Economic Progress*. For a list of the main authors of studies on services, see the Bibliography.

8. These observations have been summarized by Victor R. Fuchs in *The Service Economy* [1968] and in a series of articles by MacMahon and Worswick [1960, 1961].

9. On this point, see Stef de Jong [1983].

10. Neither available data nor the results of research undertaken to date make it possible at this time to verify the hypothesis presented in the preceding paragraph.

11. In the case of nil or negative returns on investments, the net transfer of resources on this account is also negative.

12. See in this connection the Convention for the Protection of Individuals with Regard to Automatic Processing of Personal Data, adopted by the Council of Europe in 1980 under pressure of public opinion from a large number of European democracies [1981].

13. The possibility of maintaining reservations leads to an imbalance between the obligations of various signatory governments. The absence of a dispute settlement mechanism also weakens the surveillance of the practical implementation of the provisions of the codes.

5 BASIC DATA AND TRENDS IN PRODUCTION AND TRADE IN SERVICES

The most striking fact that emerges from national accounts statistics is the large share of services in the total output of most countries, whatever their level of economic development. There is hardly a country for which this share is lower than one-fifth, and in general it is at least one-third. Table 5–1 presents average figures for three categories of countries classified according to World Bank criteria.

During the last 10 to 12 years, the average rate of growth of services output has been higher than that of gross national product (GNP) in these three main categories of countries. This contrasts with the 1960s when the reverse was true. In low-income countries and industrialized countries, the fall in the rate of growth of industrial production is essentially the cause of this reversal. Yet, the upward trend in services has also manifested itself in the economies of middle-income countries which, on the whole, were the most dynamic during the last quarter of a century.[1]

Employment figures are also significant in both developing and developed countries (table 5–2). Employment in services has increased by one-third between 1960 and 1981 in middle-income countries, whereas it has fallen by one-quarter in agriculture and has risen by one-third in industry. In industrialized countries, employment in services rose by a little less than

81

Table 5–1.   Share of Services in Gross National Product (GNP) and Average Annual Rate of Increase 1960–70 and 1970–81[1]

	Services			Industry			Agriculture			GNP	
	% of GNP in 1981 (w)	Growth in % in 1960–70 (m)	1970–81 (m)	% of GNP in 1981 (w)	Growth in % in 1960–70 (m)	1970–81 (m)	% of GNP in 1981 (w)	Growth in % in 1960–70 (m)	1970–81 (m)	Growth in % in 1960–70 (w)	1970–81 (w)
Low-income countries[2]	29	4,2	4,6	34	6,6	3,6	37	2,2	2,3	4,6	4,5
Middle-income countries[3]	48	5,5	6,1	38	7,4	6,8	14	3,4	3,0	6,0	5,6
Industrial countries[4]	61	4,6	3,6	36	5,7	2,9	3	1,4	1,6	5,1	3,0

w = weighted average.
m = median.

1. Share in current prices, growth in constant prices.
2. Thirty-four countries with a per capita income equal to or below U.S. $400 at 1981 prices.
3. Sixty countries with a per capita income above U.S. $400 including Greece, Israel, Portugal, and Yugoslavia. The richest country in this category (Trinidad and Tobago) had a per capita income of U.S. $5,670 in 1981. Excluded from this group are four high-income oil-exporting countries.
4. Nineteen market economy countries including Spain.
Source: World Bank. *World Development Report, Washington, D.C. 1983.*

Table 5–2.   Distribution of Employment by Sectors, 1960 and 1981 (Percentage of Labor Force)

	Services (w)		Industry (w)		Agriculture (w)	
	1960	1981	1960	1981	1960	1981
Low-income countries[1]	14	15	9	15	77	70
Middle-income countries[2]	23	34	15	21	62	45
Industrial countries[3]	44	56	38	38	18	6

w = weighted average.
1., 2., 3.: see notes 2., 3., and 4. to table 5–1.
Source: See table 5–1.

one-quarter, whereas it fell by two-thirds in agriculture and remained stable in industry. Only in low-income countries did employment in services remain stable in percentage terms, as all development activity was concentrated in industry where employment almost doubled, whereas a fall of 10 percent was recorded in agriculture.

The juxtaposition of production and employment data shows that apparent labor productivity in services followed different trends in the various categories of countries, as already remarked by Chenery and Syrquin [1975, figure 9, p. 52] (table 5–3).

In 1981, in low-income countries (less than U.S.$400 per head), 15 percent of the total labor force produced 29 percent of GNP in the sector of services. In average-income countries (U.S.$400 to 5,670 per capita) 34 percent of the labor force produced 48 percent of GNP, and in industrialized countries 56 percent of the labor force produced 61 percent of GNP in that sector.

What is most striking in these general statistics is that services are already important at the least advanced stages of economic development. They even show that the services sector is relatively more efficient in less-advanced countries, which runs contrary to the general perception about production conditions in those countries. This raises the question of the role of services in market mechanisms. The considerations presented on this point in the preceding chapters are confirmed by the available statistical material, however incomplete it may be.

First, it will be noted that the role of services increases as a direct function of the dimension of the market[2] on which are sold the goods produced by other sectors of the economy (agriculture, handicraft, and industry). Variations occur, notably when periods of rapid industrialization bring about a

Table 5–3.   Apparent Labor Productivity in Services, 1981[1]

Low-income Countries[2]	Middle-income Countries[3]	Industrial Countries[4]
1,9	1,4	1,1

1. The indices are calculated from the percentages appearing in tables 5–1 and 5–2.
2., 3., 4.: see table 5–1.
Source: See tables 5–1 and 5–2.

temporary lowering of the share of services in GNP, but in general the relative importance of services in total output increases steadily.

Secondly, with the exception of subsistence economies, a certain *minimum* of services seems to be necessary to establish the link between supply and demand for goods. Thus, in 1981, in no market-economy country was the share of services in GNP lower than 20 percent, and only eight countries showed a share lower than 30 percent.[3] When product markets reach a national and subsequently international dimension, and production and demand become diversified, the minimum amount of services needed in the market increases rapidly in order to face up to the growing complexity of the intermediation tasks required.

The apparent reduction of labor productivity in services in the course of economic development can easily be explained. When the production of marketable goods remains limited, there is only a need to serve local and regional markets where neither supply nor demand are very diversified. The minimum of services required for this purpose can technically be rendered by a relatively limited manpower, but the external economies produced and invoiced are still sizable. On the other hand, as economic development accelerates, the newness of tasks to be accomplished as well as the appearance of certain technical limitations to their modernization prevent the productivity of services from increasing as rapidly as the dimension of the market, which gives rise to the necessity of devoting a higher percentage of labor to service the latter.

These observations are, of course, made with all due regard being paid to the serious deficiencies of available statistics. Indeed, in many cases, particularly in developing countries, the share of GNP attributed to the services sector is estimated as a residual on the basis of expenditure data, whereas labor employed in this sector is probably only partially recorded because part of it consists of laborers without stable, full-time employment. The result is an overestimation of output in the services sector and an underestimation of factors employed by that sector, hence an overvaluation of productivity.

Another factor tends to reduce even further the significance of data on the productivity of services in developing countries. A large share of employment in this sector is perhaps nothing more than disguised unemployment. The marginal and parasitic character of certain service activities, particularly in distribution (small trade and transport activities) and in personal and domestic services,[4] is such that they cannot always be considered as autonomous sources of value-added, but rather as the counterpart of a transfer of value-added originating in the so-called productive sectors of the economy.

Goods-Services Linkages in the Economy

Since the available data are not very helpful to analyze the relationship between the share of services in GNP and the level of economic development, a qualitative analysis of this relationship may throw some light on the issue.

Certain service activities have an organic relationship with goods production because they are performed within goods producing enterprises. Other services only have a functional relationship with such production because they are produced by enterprises or individuals working independently. At different stages of economic development, certain activities which were previously exercised within goods producing enterprises are now performed outside, and vice versa. This is what we have called above the phenomena of *externalization* and *internalization* of services. For example, data processing services are more and more externalized in industrial countries, whereas traditional secretarial services (public scribes) have for a long time been internalized in modern enterprises.

The outward or inward movement of a particular service depends on a great number of factors including natural factors (for example, insularity in the case of transport), among which the most important ones appear to be the following: (1) the level of economic development and the degree of dissemination of techniques or, more precisely, the general technological development of a given economy; (2) the degree of development of merchandise trade—in other words, the scope and coherence of the market. In the long run, the processes of externalization and internalization are reversible because techniques and the market can evolve in such a way that what was economic yesterday, is less so today.[5]

Moreover, the role of services evolves with the participation of individual producers and consumers in the monetized economy, as well as with production and trade relationships that establish themselves between them.

In less-advanced countries, a high percentage of the population is occupied in "small jobs" or perform small services functions which have the appearance of being occasional. For example, porterage, small errands, cleaning work, caretaking, and domestic service do not seem to be fully integrated into existing production and distribution systems, all the less so as the labor performing these functions does not fill established posts. The instability of this labor is more often due to the fact that the small tasks which the workers concerned execute on demand only earn them a subsistence salary (sometimes indeed paid in kind) which complements the regular income earned by one or several other members of their family or extended family. Yet, such work is not always poorly paid, because the contribution of fluctuating manpower to the final value of the goods marketed can be considerable, given the general level of transport and communication technology in the countries concerned.

Traditional economies are characterized by a wide dispersion of units of production and sales outlets. This mainly reflects the low rate of organization and the narrowness of financially solvent consumer markets. In such an environment, marketing is a motive force behind material production and employment through the widening of the scope of activity of agricultural and industrial enterprises which it makes possible. Marketing activities tend consequently to be well-paid, which implies that margins of distribution are high for transporters, intermediaries, and tradesmen, all of whom belong to what, in earlier times, was called the "class of merchants." For similar reasons of technology and practicality, other auxiliary services including domestic and personal services are relatively well-paid at those stages of development. The seller of cigarettes on the street corner fulfills a function in a situation where the supermarket has no *raison d'être* because it implies a mobility of the consumer which he simply does not have. At the national level, these economic conditions are reflected in the allocation of a high proportion of total income to the sector of services as a whole, and consequently in a high ratio of services to GNP.

As the economy develops and the internal market becomes more fully integrated, the interdependence between units of production and of consumption of goods increases. Services, particularly trade, transport, and communications, establish the link between the ones and the others. In turn, services become organized, and the labor they employ becomes more stable. It is at this point that one witnesses the emergence of a full-fledged *sector* of activity distinct from handicraft, industry, and agriculture. From then on, the development of services follows its own course, creating new techniques, eventually opening new markets, which act as a stimulus to the production and marketing of goods.

In industrializing economies, the share of services in total income continues to increase but irregularly. This is due to the fact that it is subject to two conflicting influences. On the one hand, the slowdown of activity in traditional services resulting from the mechanization of work and from the improvement in communications (roads, telephones, etc.) tends to reduce the share of total product allocated to the services sector. On the other hand, the necessity to face up to the greater complexity of tasks of intermediation between producers and consumers, which accompanies the gradual widening of the market to the national and later to the international dimension, tends to stimulate the development of independent service activities.

Services in GNP

Table 5–4 shows, for a number of countries ranked by increasing order of per capita income and selected on the basis of the diversity of their structures of production but also taking into account the availability of data, the share of services as a whole and of some subsectors of service activities in GNP in 1960 and 1979.

In the period 1960–79, the share of services in GNP at current prices has risen in the 9 industrialized and in 10 of the 20 developing countries in the table. There is no systematic relationship between the rate of growth of GNP and the increase in the share of services in GNP during that period. However, given cyclical fluctuations of economic activity and the different structural evolutions of the countries concerned, in particular the rapid development of industry in some of them, the table bears witness to a general tendency of services activities as a whole to expand in line with national per capita income. This corresponds to the increased role of services in the process of market integration which, in turn, is a function of the diversification and intensification of trade mechanisms accompanying the growth of financially solvent demand.

Data available on prices of services in the same countries (table 5–5) can also be analyzed in terms of the contribution of services to the process of integration of national markets. For example, the reduced demand for traditional services (manual transport, hawker trade, domestic and personal services) in economies entering their first phase of industrialization tends to exert a downward pressure on the average prices of services. Conversely, increased demand for new services of transport, telecommunication, financing, market research, advertising, etc., in more advanced economies exert an upward pressure on the prices of these services. This is probably the reason why, as economies rise on the scale of per capita income, the average

Table 5–4. Percentage Shares of the Main Categories of Services in Gross National Product, 1960 and 1979 (in Current Prices)

Country	GNP per Head (1981 US$)	Average Annual Growth Rate of GNP (1960–81) %	Total 1960	Total 1979	Trade (Including Restaurants and Hotels) 1960	Trade (Including Restaurants and Hotels) 1979	Transport and Communications 1960	Transport and Communications 1979	Financial Services, Real Estate, Business Services, and Insurance 1960	Financial Services, Real Estate, Business Services, and Insurance 1979	Public Utilities (Electricity, Gas, and Water) 1960	Public Utilities (Electricity, Gas, and Water) 1979	Other[1] (Including Community and Personal Services) 1960	Other[1] (Including Community and Personal Services) 1979
Bangladesh	140	0,3	n.d.	37	n.d.	11*	n.d.	7	n.d.	8	n.d.	2	n.d.	9*
Burma	190	1,4	52[6]	42[5]	27*[6]	29[5]*	7[6]	3[5]	26,8	‑[2,5]	16,7	‑[2,5]	17*[6,8]	10*[5]
Burundi	230	2,4	n.d.	28	n.d.	8	n.d.	3	n.d.	‑[2]	n.d.	n.d.	n.d.	17
India	260	1,4	29	37	9	15	5	5	5	6	1	2	9	9
Sierra Leone	320	0,4	38[6]	42[5]	13[6]	13[5]	8[6]	11[5]	6[6]	9[5]	1[6]	1[5]	10[6]	8[5]
Pakistan	350	2,8	40	43	13*	13	6	7	6	6	1	2	14*	15*
Kenya	420	2,9	46[6]	44	10*[6]	9	8[6]	5	9[6,9]	11	2[6]	2	17*[6,9]	17
Zambia	600	0,0	33[6]	45	12[6]	11	4[6]	6	4[6]	10	1[6]	2	12[6]	16
Egypt	650	3,5	42	42	10[10]	17	7	7	5[11]	2	‑[2]	‑[2]	20	16
Thailand	770	4,6	42	46	18	22	7	7	5	7	1	1	11	9
Philippines	790	2,8	40	39	11*	16	4	4	7[9]	9	1	1	17*[9]	9
Nicaragua	860	0,6	56	51	22*	24*	6	5	12[9]	8[9]	1	1	15*[9]	12*[9]
Nigeria	870	3,5	26	37[13]	12*	21[13]	5	3[13]	4[12]	2[13]	1	1[13]	4*[12]	10[13]
Ecuador	1,180	4,3	37	41	10	15	4	5	9	9	1	1	13	12
Colombia	1,380	3,2	43	43	15*	17*	7	6	8[9]	8[9]	1	2	12*[9]	10[9]
Turkey	1,540	3,5	38	48	9*	13*	7	9	8[9]	8[9]	1	2	13*[9]	16*[9]
Korea (Republic of)	1,700[4]	6,9[4]	43	40	13	15	5	6	8	6	1	2	15	11
Brazil	2,220	5,1	43	46	12*	12*	5	4	8	16[9]	1	2	17*	12*[9]
Mexico	2,250	3,8	57	54	34	30	3	3	9	6	1	1	10	14
Venezuela	4,220	2,4	n.d.	52	n.d.	9	n.d.	11	n.d.	15	n.d.	1[14]	n.d.	16
Singapore	5,240	7,4	78	66	33	26	14	13	11	14	2	2	18	11
Spain	5,640	4,2	40	55[5]	9	17[5]	6	7[5]	6[5,9,15]	‑[2,5]	2	2[5]	17[9,15]	29[2,5,9,15]
Italy	6,960	3,6	47	52	13	15	6	7	10	‑[2]	3	n.d.	15	31
United Kingdom	9,110	2,1	48	56	11*	9*	8	7	9[9]	13[9]	2	3	18[9]	24[9]
Japan	10,080	6,3	49	59	17*	13*	8	7	9	15	2	2	13*	22*
France	12,190	3,8	n.d.	56	n.d.	12	n.d.	6	n.d.	16	n.d.	2	n.d.	20
United States	12,820	2,3	63	68	17	17	7	6	17	20	3[16]	3[16]	19[17]	22[17]

Germany (Federal Republic of)	13,450	3,2	42	51	13	10	6	6	7[18]	9[18]	2	n.d.	14[18]	26[18]
Norway	14,060	3,5	56	59	18*	14*	16	11	5[9]	11[9]	3	4	14**[9]	19**[9]
Sweden	14,870	2,6	46[6]	55	10[6]	10	5[6]	6	12[6]	12	2	2	17[6]	25

1. Community services and private sector social services, plus personal services. In certain cases, marked with an asterix*, this category also includes restaurant and hotel services. The data on "other" services being generally very incomplete, the percentages in this column are estimated as residuals using as total the data for the service sector as a whole published by the World Bank. Although some more recent figures exist for certain countries, it has seemed preferable, for purposes of comparison, to use 1979 data.

2. Included in "Others."

3. 1980 at 1980 prices.

4. *Source:* IBRD, *World Development Report*, Washington, D.C. 1982.

5. 1978.

6. 1965.

7. Electricity only. The other services in this category are included in "Others."

8. Financial services are included in "Others."

9. Business services are included in "Others."

10. Including financial services and insurance.

11. See footnote 10.

12. Real estate services are included in "Others."

13. 1977.

14. Excluding gas.

15. Real estate services other than rentals are included in "Others."

16. Including health and similar services.

17. Including services provided by public enterprises.

18. Publication services, business services, and real estate services other than rental are included in "Others."

n.a.: Not available for 1960 or for a neighboring year.

N.B.: Figures being rounded to the nearest unit, the sum of the columns does not always equal the corresponding total. In certain cases, not indicated in the table, the definition of categories is somewhat different from that used by the United Nations. In general, this affects the distribution of different services between the categories of columns 6 and 8.

Sources: United Nations. *Yearbook of National Accounts Statistics, 1979* and 1980, vol. 1, table 1.10. World Bank. *World Development Report, 1983*, for GNP data except Korea (see footnote 4).

Table 5–5. Implicit Price Indices for Services, 1980 (National Currencies, at 1975 Prices) (1960 = 100)

(1) Country	(2) GNP Deflator	(3) Wholesale and Retail Trade	(4) Transport and Communications	(5) Other Services
Bangladesh[1]	264	187	248	280
Burma[3]	230	293	139	n.d.
Burundi[4]	284	320	319	355
India	413	492	319	329
Sierra Leone[9]	338	460	356	194
Pakistan	458	488	485	436
Kenya[6]	286	418	224	225
Zambia[3]	342	404	361	316
Egypt[1]	328	485	203	134
Thailand	299	351	288	259
Philippines	632	505	540	588
Nicaragua[3]	241	288	271	254
Nigeria	452	461	312	252
Ecuador[1]	315	286	349	308
Colombia	2,404	2,885	1,792	1,920
Turkey	3,997	3,435	3,107	3,130
Korea (Republic of)	2,869	2,994	910	3,847
Brazil	n.d.	n.d.	n.d.	n.d.
Mexico	713	631	516	884
Venezuela[8]	335	308	268	350[4]
Singapore	189	175	128	179
Spain	755	888[9]	429[9]	1,085[9]
Italy	615	494	513	401[4]
United Kingdom[4]	385	382	325	421
Japan[4]	200	161	199	261
France	378	333	324	564
United States[4]	197	186	177	197
Germany (Fed. Rep.)	236	209	202	353
Norway	350	340	184	433
Sweden	378	431	327	487

1. 1972 = 100.
2. 1962 = 100.
3. 1978.
4. 1970 = 100.
5. 1963 = 100.
6. 1964 = 100.
7. 1965 = 100.
8. 1968 = 100.
9. 1979.

Source: United Nations. *Yearbook of National Accounts Statistics, 1980 and 1981*, vols. I and II, tables 10B (1980) and 9B (1981).

increase in the prices of "other" services in table 5–5 tends to overtake that of other categories of services and of GNP as a whole. It must be recognized, however, that the available data refer to categories which are too widely defined and too fragmentary to allow reliable conclusions.

Figures in table 5–4 relating to subsectors of activity give some supplementary indications of the *minimum amount* of services required in an economy to permit the market to operate. In this regard, the most significant categories of services are trade and transport and communications. The table shows that there is no systematic gap between low-income and high-income countries with regard to the share that each of these two categories of services holds in national product. Nor is there any systematic variation between countries with comparable incomes but of different geographical dimensions such as Zambia and Thailand or Philippines and Nicaragua. On the other hand, the minimum amounts differ between the two services categories. In the case of trade, the minimum share of GNP is *8 or 9 percent* whatever the level of economic development; for transport and communications, it is *2 or 3 percent*, irrespective of the economic structure or rate of growth of the countries concerned.

For the other subsectors of services activities, table 5–4 shows a tendency for their share in GNP to increase in line with per capita income, especially if one compares developed with other countries. This trend is fairly marked for financial services and business services and a little less for the various social and personal services appearing in the last column of the table. Abstracting from extreme cases, the minimum share of financial services can be set at *5 to 6 percent* of GNP and that of residual services at *8 or 9 percent*, representing amounts necessary for the operation of the economy at any particular level of development.

If the minimum amounts given above are added together for 30 countries, the totals fall within a range of *23 to 27 percent* as the share of all services in GNP, excluding public utilities, which correspond more or less to the minimum amounts appearing in World Bank statistics relating to 124 countries [see *World Development Report, 1983*, table 3(4)].

Much more detailed data will be necessary before clearer conclusions can be drawn on the significance of these minima. In particular, the category of financial services, etc., covers heterogeneous activities (banking, insurance architects, accounting, engineering, to name only a few), each of which varies more or less systematically with the production structure and level of development of individual countries. It will probably be necessary to wait until statistical methods have been improved before more useful indications can be obtained on the value produced by the different economic agents working in the multiple branches of this category.

Data on employment in the services sector provide complementary information on the role of services in the economy, but they are also incomplete. Thus, the available statistics do not cover employment in services rendered within goods producing enterprises and whose value-added is included in that of goods, nor employment in services provided *by* goods producing enterprises to their customers (after-sales services, technology transfers, etc.).

One way of better apprehending the problem is to compare labor force statistics relating to the sectors of industry, agriculture, and services as these sectors are usually defined, with statistics on labor employed by profession, irrespective of the type of enterprise that employs it, and including non-salaried workers. The relevant data are given in tables 5–6 and 5–7.

If it is true that a more or less important share of value-added in industry and agriculture is attributable to services supplied within these two large sectors of activity, sectoral labor statistics should show *higher* numbers of employed in these sectors than statistics relating to direct production workers. The larger the gap between the two figures, the more intermediation services between producers and consumers can be internalized in industrial and agricultural enterprises.[6] In the services sector, the converse is true: sectoral data are *lower* than data by type of professional activity when intermediation services are internalized in industrial and agricultural enterprises.

The available data do not permit a comparison of these two statistical series for all the countries listed in table 5–4. However, for industrial countries, the relationship between data by sector and data by profession confirms the hypothesis of internalization in industry, albeit not in agriculture. For developing countries the relationships vary more markedly from one country to another and do not permit any useful generalization.

Another way of analyzing the statistics is to evaluate the degree of externalization of services activities on the basis of the evolution of the share of certain professional categories in total employment. Table 5–6 shows that activities with a high cultural content (columns 5 to 7 of the table) hold a relatively large share of the total in developed countries, both in absolute terms and by comparison with developing countries. This is most notable for the group "management and professions," and it is probably related to the development of new independent services activities. Here again, however, the data are not sufficiently precise to permit a definitive judgment of the case.

The category of "service workers" in table 5–6 is a special case, in the sense that it comprises acitivities such as domestic and personal services which may serve as safety valves in periods of sluggish economic activity. If this interpretation is correct, the table then shows that developing countries

Table 5–6. Structure of Labor Force by Professions, 1980 (Percentages)

Country	Production and Related Workers, Transport Equipment Operators & Laborers[2]	Agriculture, Animal Husbandry, etc.	Service Workers[1]	Sales Workers	Clerical & Related Workers	Administrative, Managerial, & Professional Workers	Not Elsewhere Specified[3]	Total[4]
Pakistan	25	51	4	10	3	4	4	100
Egypt	22	40	8	6	8	11	4	100
Thailand	11	73	3	8	2	3	–	100
Philippines	19	51	8	11	4	7	1	100
Ecuador	23	46	7	8	4	6	6	100
Turkey	21	64	4	3	3	5	–	100
Brazil	19	44	8	8	5	8	8	100
Singapore	38	3	10	14	14	13	8	100
Japan	37	10	6	14	17	12	3	100
United States	31	3	13	6	18	26	3	100
Germany (Fed. Rep.)	36	5	11	8	19	16	4	100
Norway	33	8	12	10	10	24	3	100
Sweden	30	5	13	8	12	28	3	100

1. Sections 5–0 to 5–9 of SICP-1968, covering essentially miscellaneous services, domestic and personal services, and restaurant and hotel services.
2. Including telecommunication workers.
3. Including school leavers and unemployed workers (?).
4. The total does not necessarily correspond to the sum of columns 1 to 8 due to rounding of data to the nearest unit. The figures of column 8 should be read with particular caution due to the existence of different definitions of unemployment from one country to another.

Source: ILO, Yearbook of Labor Statistics, 1980–1982, table 2C.

Table 5–7. Labor Force Engaged in the Production of Goods, by Sector and by Profession, 1980 (Percentages of Total Labor Force)

Country	A. By Sector			B. By Profession[1]			C. Memorandum Item	
	Industry	Agriculture	Total	Industry	Agriculture	Total	Services by Sector (100–A3)	Services by Professions (100–B3)
Pakistan	20	57	77	21	51	72	23	28
Egypt	30	50	80	19	39	58	20	42
Thailand	9	76	85	6	73	79	15	21
Philippines	17	46	63	16	51	67	37	33
Ecuador	17	52	69	19	46	65	31	35
Turkey	13	54	67	15	64	79	33	21
Brazil	24	30	54	16	44	60	46	40
Singapore	39	2	41	29	3	32	59	68
Japan	39	12	51	31	10	41	49	59
United States	32	2	34	26	3	29	66	71
Germany (Fed. Rep.)	46	4	50	31	5	36	50	64
Norway	37	7	44	23	8	31	56	69
Sweden	34	5	39	25	5	30	61	70

1. For agriculture, the data used are those of table 5–6. For industry the data of 5–6 have been adjusted for the estimated percentage of labor employed in transport and communications, the latter being calculated from the corresponding figures of table 5–4 and the data in table 5–3.
Source: Employment by sector: World Bank. World Development Report, 1983; Employment by profession: table 5–6.

do not have the exclusivity of disguised unemployment in the tertiary sector.

To conclude this section, it is appropriate to return briefly to the question of the productivity of services. Research undertaken by Victor Fuchs [1969] has identified five main causes of the more rapid increase of employment in services than in industry in the United States: (1) technological development (replacement of labor by machines and economies of scale) is more rapid in industry; (2) capital formation grows more rapidly in industry; (3) hours worked are shorter in services; (4) labor is more qualified in industry; (5) production increases more rapidly in services. These observations are interesting, but they fail to explain why the sector of services, where apparent productivity is lower than in industry (see Fuchs, 1969; Smith, 1972], can *usefully* absorb excess labor rather than this labor remaining unemployed. In particular, it seems that other explanations than the lower degree of qualification of labor in services can be advanced.

Table 5–3 has shown that as one moves up the scale of per capita incomes, apparent productivity in services diminishes. If we follow Fuch's reasoning, this could be attributed to the gradual replacement of unskilled labor by skilled labor in industry. But we can also assume much more simply that as services become organized and labor employed in this sector is stabilized, the statistics of employment become more complete and this produces an apparent reduction in productivity.

In addition, beyond the initial phase of organization, in average-income countries which are entering into a period of industrialization and extension of their internal markets, the rate of increase of the labor force employed in services slows down [Fuchs, 1969, p. 146; see also Chenery and Syrquin, 1975, p. 50] before resuming its preceding growth path. One would therefore expect productivity to increase in this intermediate phase. If it does not increase, it is perhaps because the multiplication of independent service enterprises linked to the extension of the internal market deprives the first among them to have been established of the scarcity rents which they enjoyed initially, thus gradually bringing down their rates of return to a more "competitive level." These considerations, like others presented in the present study, should lead to a reexamination of the standard hypothesis[7] that the increase in the share of services in GNP brings about a secular decrease in the rate of growth of the economy.

Services in International Trade

Services that are internalized in goods producing enterprises are not traded as such: they are integrated or embodied in manufactured goods of which they increase the value. The external trade of a country includes, there-fore, a greater or lesser amount of services embodied in goods, according to the nature of the goods traded and the conditions under which they are produced or manufactured. This aspect of trade has commended little atten-tion among economists up to now, and it is not included among the explana-tions given of the more rapid increase in world trade than in world output in the post-war period.[8] The technological factor has only been analyzed from the point of view of the impact of innovation on the reduction in the cost of transport and communication, on the rate of consumption of raw materials per unit of manufactured product, and on product diversification.

Yet, what characterizes distant trade is its tendency to eliminate as much as possible from commercial interchange the heaviest components of traded goods and to increase as much as possible the proportion of value-added traded. The trend toward higher value/weight ratios of goods is weakened by reductions in transport costs, but it remains fundamental because the attractiveness of goods depends on work embodied in them and not just on the materials of which they are made. This is in fact the only real meaning of the effect of product differentiation on trade, although it has not been dis-cussed as such by international trade theoreticians: they speak of gains from scale economies which result from specialization of production, but not of the research and development or knowledge content of traded goods. In addition to the fact that it is this content which gives most of their value to goods, it is easily transferable to distant places because it weighs nothing, and it makes the goods themselves more accessible because it facilitates their use. These characteristics of distant trade largely explain why the value of world trade has expanded more rapidly than world production in a period when technological progress was more rapid than ever before. More and more, exports from industrial countries, which account for more than half of world trade, are composed of high technology goods, while the manufacture of the heavier components of these goods is subcontracted to developing countries.

There exist no detailed statistics on the content of services in goods entering international trade. Value/weight ratios are about the only useful indicator, and the data necessary to calculate them exist only for certain countries and certain goods. There is, therefore, a great amount of work that remains to be done to identify the role of individual countries or production sectors in the international exchange of knowledge and technology. This research can only be successful if it benefits from the assistance of the nation-al statistical offices of all major trading countries. It falls outside the scope of this book, which can hope only to contribute to greater awareness of the problem.

Services as Items of Trade

As soon as a service ceases to be an integral part of a goods producing process, it can be traded like any good. It is therefore *externalized* and *organized* services, in the sense in which these terms have been used here, which enter into international trade as distinct products. However, they differ from other products in that they are intangible. Moreover, since the substance and value of services are contained in the very act of rendering the services, traded services are by definition finite (with the exception of stored information) and nontransferable from one consumer to another. For this reason, most services cannot be supplied unless the supplier and the user are located in the same place at the same time. In order to increase the geographical scope of its activities, a service enterprise is thus often obliged to multiply its units of production and not only its sales outlets. This does not

Table 5–8.   World Exports and Imports of Services and Other Current Account Items, 1981[1] (Million U.S. Dollars)

		Exports	Imports
A.	Services (nonfactor)[2]	361,5	387,2
	of which: transport	134,2	164,8
	travel	99,1	99,4
	others	128,2	123,0
B.	Interest and returns on capital	223,2	256,9
C.	Transfers	115,7	115,8
	of which: private	41,9	31,4
	public (grants)	32,8	50,6
	other public transfers	41,0	33,8
D.	Goods	1,676,5	1,658,8
E.	Total	2,376,9	2,418,7

1. The "world" includes most member countries of IMF plus Switzerland. Excluded are the USSR, China, and Eastern European countries other than Romania and Yugoslavia.

2. There is no correspondence between the classification of table 1–1 (page 4) and that of the International Monetary Fund. However, almost all the services of table 1–1 are included in whole or in part in the category "other services" of the IMF. Other services are distributed as follows: "transport" includes items 1 and 2 (maritime transport, air transport, and auxiliary transport services) and part of item 4 (freight insurance); "travel" includes all tourist spending not appearing in table 1–1

Source: Committee on Invisible Exports. *World Invisible Trade*, table 1. London, June 1983.

Table 5–9. Services Balances of the 35 Main Trading Countries in this Sector, 1981 (Million U.S. Dollars)

(1) Country	(2) Transport	(3) Travel	(4) Other Services	(5) Total Columns 2 to 4	(6) Memorandum Item: Interest and Other Returns on Capital
I. Developed countries					
Austria	−234	2,761	1,008	3,535	−462
Australia	−38	−671	−1,968	−2,677	−2,457
Canada	−71	−886	−1,456	−2,413	−9,557
EEC[1]	−83	−4,131	13,116	8,902	−4,849
Belgium-Luxembourg	379	1,098	1,002	2,479	−205
Denmark	438	−35	827	1,230	−1,980
France	−1,341	1,496	3,700	3,855	775
Germany (Fed. Rep.)	−1,797	−11,432	−2,532	−15,761	−2,699
Greece	133	1,547	745	2,425	–
Ireland[2]	199	−22	100	277	−260
Italy	−1,293	5,831	669	5,207	−3,208
Netherlands	2,521	−2,053	586	1,054	−698
United Kingdom	678	−561	8,019	8,136	3,426
Finland	−231	100	255	124	−981
Japan	−3,164	−3,888	−7,443	−14,495	−5,677
Norway	2,546	−820	−230	1,496	−981
Portugal	−165	783	13	631	−722
South Africa	−1,065	−143	−875	−2,083	−2,098
Spain	591	5,763	−266	6,088	−3,132

Sweden	495	−1,266	1,031	260	−1,389
Switzerland	−284	1,311	764	1,791	5,141
United States	−948	706	7,414	7,172	46,072
II. Developing countries					
Argentina	−270	1,021	−269	1,560	−3,306
Brazil	−1,692	−174	−591	−2,457	−10,327
Chile	−619	−39	−150	−808	−1,428
Egypt	479	242	−561	160	−497
India	−1,281	980	335	34	836
Israel	−178	347	−98	71	−422
Korea (Republic of)	−79	6	2,532	2,459	−3,804
Kuwait	−427	−671	89	−1,187	2,289
Mexico	−1,887	67	719	−1,101	−8,741
Panama	313	106	296	715	94
Saudi Arabia	−5,499	−1,188	−3,177	−9,864	−6,848
Singapore	1,605	1,367	2,013	4,985	−428
Taiwan	−1,116	104	−179	−1,191	−290
Venezuela	−1,058	−2,098	−652	−3,808	821
Yugoslavia	−141	1,515	47	1,421	−1,387

1. Gross figures including intracommunity trade.
2. 1980.

Source: Committee on Invisible Exports. *World Invisible Trade*, June 1983. The statistics published in this source are taken from the IMF.

raise any particular problem where there are no restraints to the establishment of new units of production. When such restraints exist, service enterprises cannot develop beyond the limits imposed by saturation of demand on their local market. Now, whereas most countries allow domestic enterprises to establish freely anywhere on their territory, the same treatment is rarely accorded to foreign enterprises.

Consequently, international trade in services faces two difficulties: (1) the intangibility of services, insofar as the nature of service acts make their sale in distant markets impossible; and (2) the fact that this technical handicap is difficult or impossible to overcome given the barriers imposed by many countries to the establishment of foreign enterprises on their territory.

Statistical data on international trade in services are fragmentary and not sufficiently broken down, partly because of the intangible character of the transactions, partly because of the little attention which has been paid up to now to this type of trade by national and international statisticians. Moreover, there are no precise figures in existence on returns from the foreign activities of branches and subsidiaries of service enterprises, since these return figures are usually included without distinction of origin in the item "interest, dividends, and other returns from capital" of the balance of payments.[9] It is necessary to rely on more or less aggregated data based in most cases on the balance of payments statistics published by the International Monetary Fund (IMF).

Table 5–8 shows the value of world exports of services distributed according to the IMF classification and compared with total trade, properly speaking, and with total current transactions. In 1980, world services exports amounted to 271.4 billion SDR (Special Drawing Rights of the IMF), or about U.S.$350 billion. This represented 17.3 percent of total world exports of goods and services and 14.9 percent of world receipts on current transactions (that is to say, including returns on capital and transfers). It will be noted that there are considerable discrepancies between the figures for world exports and imports of transport and "other" services, which can only be explained by deficiencies in the collection of the relevant data on one side or the other of the account.

This anomaly must be taken into account when analyzing net flows of services as a whole or of specific categories of services for individual countries. Nevertheless, national data on service flows are interesting in that they reflect fairly well the influence of a number of factors on the respective position of each country.

An examination of the current balances of the countries having the highest amount of trade in services (table 5–9) reveals significant differences among them. Apart from natural factor endowments,[10] economic history, geographical location, structure and nature of exports (in particular the share of primary commodities in total exports), and movements of migrant workers, throw light on individual deficits or surpluses. For example, in the case of shipping, given that developing countries own only 10 percent of the world fleet whereas they export 60 percent of the commodities transported by ship,[11] it is not surprising to see that most of these countries have a deficit on trade in shipping services.

In addition, given that for oil and bulk cargo developing countries own only 16 percent of the world fleet while they export 90 percent of the commodities transported, it is not surprising to see oil-exporting countries such as Saudi Arabia, Iran, Venezuela, and Mexico, or countries like Argentina which are major exporters of dry cargo (e.g., cereals, meat), with large deficits under this item.

Finally, table 5–10 presents more detailed data for the countries appearing in table 5–4.[12] Among the developing countries listed, only Korea and Brazil show a surplus under the item "shipping." Egypt and Singapore are the only countries to show an important surplus under the item "travel and other transport." As far as Egypt is concerned, Suez Canal dues largely compensate for net expenditures for the transport of Egyptian exports and imports. In the case of Singapore, port charges and passenger air traffic provide the important receipts that compensate for the shipping deficit. Abstracting from these particular cases, it is remarkable that, whereas in general developing countries show a deficit in shipping for the reasons indicated in the preceding paragraph, there does not seem to be a systematic evolution of the deficit in relation to their respective level of development.[13] The same observation holds for developed countries, whose comparative advantages are not brought out very clearly by the general data available. It is therefore appropriate to treat with caution any general conclusion drawn from the comparison of aggregate data classified along North-South lines.

The other two categories of services in table 5–10 which deserve particular attention are travel and workers' remittances. As we have seen previously, workers' remittances are not "services," properly speaking, and sales to tourists do not only involve services. However, these flows have an important impact on the balance of payments on current account of many countries. Like other invisible flows, including interest and returns of capital, they serve to compensate for the deficit on merchandise trade account, which corresponds to a deficit in national goods production, or on the contrary they oblige countries to maintain a surplus in the production of goods to ensure their financing. (For example, this is how the Federal Republic of Germany finances the tourist expenditures of its nationals abroad.)

Tables 5–11 and 5–12 present a last set of figures which give an idea of the

Table 5–10. Net Flows of Current Transactions in Services, 1981 (Million U.S. Dollars)

(1) Country	(2) Shipping	(3) Travel and Other Transport	(4) Tourism	(5) Other Private Services	(6) Total Columns 2 to 5	(7) Workers' Remittances
Bangladesh	-279	6	-12	402	-245	386
Burma	-25	-21	6	19	-21	5
India[2]	-703	-180	713	164	-6	1,301
Sierra Leone[3]	-37	26	4	-12	-19	8
Pakistan	-504	-176	21	62	-595	2,194
Kenya	-189	217	203	20	251	12
Zambia	-136	-75	-39	-90	-340	164[2]
Egypt	-880	1,360	243	-561	162	2,231
Thailand	-916	-2	705	20	-153	554
Philippines	-427	-112	216	221	-103	323
Nicaragua	-2,111	-4[4]	-781	-1,651	-4,543	-441
Nigeria	-1,453	-90	-724	-1,473	-3,739	-441
Ecuador	-140	-77	-119	-114	-450	n.d.
Colombia	0	-176	114	58	-4	90
Turkey	-978	53	282	237	-406	2,582
Korea (Republic of)	-768	-848	6	1,268[5]	-74	425
Brazil	301	-1,993	-175	-592	-2,459	186
Mexico	-1,087	-801	68	1,238	-581	125
Venezuela	-1,178	119	-2,098	-652	-3,809	-383

Singapore	−679	2,283	1,367	2,013	4,983	−48
Spain	−184	775	5,762	8	6,361	1,698
Italy	−1,608	312	5,831	−391	4,144	1,407
United Kingdom	1,174	−500	−560	7,763	7,877	−562
Japan	4,504	−7,665	−3,891	−6,167	−13,219	−200
France	−967	−357	1,496	4,463[6]	4,615	−2,275
United States	2,700	1,757	708	1,120	884	−637
Germany (Fed. Rep.)	−637	−1,144	−11,438	−790	−14,009	−4,905
Norway	4,757	−2,841	−820	−215	882	−29
Sweden	1,449	−953	−1,266	1,090[7]	320	−244

1. Including freight insurance. Other insurance services are included in column 5.

2. 1979.

3. 1980.

4. Included in column 2.

5. Detailed data are as follows: construction and engineering services, 1589; management services, −57; other services, −510.

6. Detailed data are as follows: construction and engineering services, 1887; insurance (other than freight insurance), −57; processing and repair services, 85; research and technical cooperation services, 1902; other, 850.

7. Detailed data are as follows: advertising, −19; brokerage expenses, −390; communications, −29; insurance (other than freight insurance) −203; other, −1,046; not elsewhere identified, 2,776.

Sources: IMF. Balance of Payments Statistics, vol. 33, Yearbook, Part I, 1982; IMF. Balance of Payments Manual. Washington, D.C., 1977.

Table 5–11.   The 25 Main Exporters of Services in 1980: International Comparisons (Million U.S. Dollars)

(1) Country	(2) Value of Exports of Services	(3) Value of Returns from Investment	(4) Value of Exports of Goods	(5) Net Flows of Services	(6) Exports of Services as a Percentage of GNP (%)	(7) Exports of Services in Percent of Exports of Goods (%)
United States	34.9	70.2	224.3	6.0	1.4	15.6
United Kingdom	34.2	17.1	110.9	9.8	6.5	30.9
France	33.0	18.4	107.6	5.5	5.1	30.7
Germany (Fed. Rep.)	31.9	8.5	185.5	−17.9	3.9	17.2
Italy	22.4	5.3	76.8	6.2	5.7	29.2
Japan	18.9	7.2	126.8	−13.4	1.8	14.9
Netherlands	17.7	10.0	67.5	0.2	10.5	26.2
Belgium	14.5	17.6	55.2	0.5	12.1	26.3
Spain	11.7	0.2	20.5	6.3	5.6	56.9
Austria	10.8	2.5	17.2	5.1	14.0	62.6
Switzerland	8.4	n.d.	29.3	1.9	8.3	28.9
Sweden	7.5	0.8	30.7	0.5	6.0	24.3
Mexico	7.4	1.0	16.2	0.2	4.0	45.8
Norway	7.3	0.5	18.7	0.3	12.7	39.2
Canada	7.0	2.9	67.6	−2.5	2.7	10.3

Singapore	5.9	n.d.	18.2	3.1	54.1	32.7
Korea (Republic of)	4.5	0.3	17.2	0.6	7.7	26.1
Yugoslavia	4.5	0.2	9.0	−0.7	7.1	49.9
Greece	4.0	*	4.1	2.6	9.9	97.2
Saudi Arabia	3.7	n.d.	100.7	−8.0	3.2	3.7
Australia	3.5	0.7	21.7	−2.5	2.5	16.2
Israel	3.2	0.7	5.8	0.4	15.9	55.8
South Africa	3.0	0.4	25.5	−1.7	3.8	11.8
Finland	2.8	0.2	14.1	*	5.6	19.6
Egypt	2.3	0.3	3.9	0.1	9.8	60.2

* Less than 50 million dollars.

Note: Data in SDR's and nominal values in national currencies have been converted into dollars at current exchange rates. The "world" comprises the member countries of the IMF which have supplied data for the years 1970 and 1980. Exports of services exclude intergovernmental transactions and returns on investments. Returns on investments cover returns on direct and portfolio investment, but not government income from abroad.

Source: IMF. *Balance of Payments Statistics, International Financial Statistics*, various issues; *U.S. National Study on Services*, Washington, D.C., 1982.

Table 5–12.   World, Main Production, and Trade Aggregates[1]

	Average Annual Rate of Increase, 1970–1980 (Percentages)	Value in 1980 (Billion U.S. Dollars)
Exports of services	18.7	350
Exports of goods	20.4	1,650
Returns on investments	22.4	225
Gross Domestic Product	14.2	9,389

1. See notes to table 5–11.

role played by services in the economic activity of main service exporting countries and in world trade. These figures are interesting because they show that the definition of trade as the act of selling and buying goods has been overtaken by events.

Notes

1. In the period 1950–70, calculations made in respect of 100 countries showed that the share of services is bell-shaped in intermediate developing countries: following an initial rise the share drops to a "normal" level, only to increase again at a regular rate in high-income industrial countries. In this regard, see the analysis of economic structures at different levels of development by Hollis Chenery and Moises Syrquin [1975], in particular the diagram on p. 36 and p. 174–177.

2. This term covers both the notion of spatial extension of the market as well as its absorption capacity, which depends on the financially solvent demand of consumers.

3. See World Bank, *World Development Report, 1983*, table 3 of the Commentary. Central-ly planned economies have a different accounting system for service activities, which makes it difficult to compare their statistics with those of other countries.

4. The traditional "parasitic" activities of this type tend to disappear in industrial countries, just like handicraft, but new service activities appear whose parasitic character, albeit not always recognized as such, is no less evident: hostesses, chauffeurs, ushers, commercial and financial intermediaries of all kinds, journalists, etc. Moreover, on this subject, it is recalled that in chapter 2, the theory of disguised unemployment in relation to services has been questioned. See also the next section below.

5. For example, the progress of literacy on one hand, and the fall in the price of typewriters on the other, have permitted the integration of secretarial services into commercial and other enterprises, whereas the emergence of new text-processing machines which are expensive and require the use of specialized personnel could, in the future, lead to a new externalization of secretarial services of the most repetitive kind.

6. It will be noted, however, that the gap may be biased upward due to the fact that data by sector include the unemployed whereas data by profession do not.

7. See, for example, Baumol [1967] and Fuchs [1969].

8. In this connection, see the study by R. Blackhurst, N. Marian, and J. Tumlir [1977], first chapter.

9. Relevant data can sometimes be found in specialized professional publications, but they are generally incomplete and rarely followed up. A special study carried out in 1981 for the United States government [Economic Consulting Services, 1981] gives a better view of the problem as it relates to the activities of American enterprises abroad, without, however, providing more than estimates of the returns in question. The statistical problem of estimating the sales of services by branches of foreign firms has also been carefully analyzed in a recent Study by UNCTAD [Conference des Nations Unies . . . , 1983], which gives some indications of the flows concerned.

10. According to André Sapir and Ernest Lutz (61), factor endowments play the same role in trade in services as they do in trade in goods. The analysis presented in chapters 2 and 3 raises certain doubts on this point. The study by Sapir and Lutz, albeit very interesting, fails to dispel all these doubts. Their correlations between service flows and some very general indicators of production costs give common sense results, but do not provide convincing proof of their starting hypothesis.

11. See J. Nusbaumer [1981, p. 221].

12. Since the IMF categories do not correspond to those of the United Nations, the data in this table are not comparable to those of table 5–4.

13. Which tends to contradict the conclusions reached by Sapir and Lutz (see note 10 above).

BIBLIOGRAPHY

Abramowitz, *Resource and Output Trends in the U.S. Since 1870*, National Bureau of Economic Research, Occasional Paper 53. New York, 1957.

Amin, Samir. *Le développement inégal*. Paris: Les editions de Minuit, 1973.

Balassa, Bela. *A "Stages" Approach to Comparative Advantage*, World Bank Staff Working Paper n° 256. Washington, D.C., May, 1977.

Banque mondiale. *Rapport sur le développement dans le monde, 1983*. Paris: Economica, 1983.

Barrère, Alain. *La crise n'est pas ce que l'on croit*. Paris: Economica, 1981.

Bauchet, Pierre. *L'Economie du transport international de marchandises, air et mer*. Paris: Economica, 1982.

Baumol, W. J. "Macroeconomics of Unbalanced Growth." *The American Economic Review*: June, 1967.

Becker, Gary. "Investment in Human Capital: A Theoretical Analysis." *The Journal of Political Economy*: October, 1962.

Bell, Daniel. *The Coming of the Post-Industrial Society; A Venture in Social Forecasting*. London: Harmsworth Press Ltd., 1976.

Bennett, W. A., and Tucker, K. A. *Structural Determinants of the Size of the Service Sector: An International Comparison*, Working Paper N. 4. Canberra: Bureau of Industry Economics, 1979.

Blackhurst, Richard, Marian, Nicolas, and Tumlir, Ian. *Libéralisation des échanges commerciaux, protectionnisme et interdépendance*. Geneva: GATT, November, 1977.

Braudel, Fernand. *Civilisation matérielle, économie et capitalisme, XVe-XVIIIe siècle*, 3 vol. Paris: Armand Colin, 1979.

Derek, W. A., Blades, W., Johnston, Derek D., and Marezewski, Witold. *Le secteur des services dans les pays en voie de développement*. Paris: Centre de développement, Organisation de coopération et de développement économiques (OCDE), 1974.

Chamberlin, E. H. *The Theory of Monopolistic Competition*. Cambridge, MA: Harvard University Press, 1933.

Channon, Derek F. *The Service Industries; Strategy, Structure and Financial Performance*. London: Macmillan, 1978.

Chenery, Hollis B., and Syrquin, Moises. *Patterns of Economic Development, 1950–1970*. London: Oxford University Press, 1975.

Clark, Colin. *Les conditions du progrès économique*. Paris: P.U.F., 1960.

Conférence des Nations Unies pour le Commerce et le Développement (CNUCED). Production et commerce des services, document TD/B/941, 1 March, 1983.

Conseil de l'Europe. *Convention pour la protection des personnes à l'égard du traitement automatisé des données à caractère personnel*. Strasbourg, 28 January, 1981.

de Jong, Stef J. M. Chr. *Transborder Data Flows: An Enquiry into the Mouldings of a Policy*. Geneva: Mémoire de diplôme, Institut Universitaire d'études européennes, September, 1983.

Deakin, B. M., and George, K. D. "Goods and Services." *London and Cambridge Economic Bulletin*: March, 1965.

————. *Productivity Trends in the Service Industries*. Cambridge: Cambridge University Press, 1969.

Deakin, B. M., and Seward, T. *Productivity in Transport, A Study of Employment, Capital, Output, Productivity and Technical Change*. Cambridge: Cambridge University Press, 1969.

Denison, Edward F. *Why Growth Rates Differ: Postwar Experience in Nine Western Countries*. Washington, D.C.: Brookings Institution, 1967.

————. *Accounting for United States Economic Growth, 1929–1979*. Washington, D.C.: The Brookings Institution, 1974.

————. *Accounting for Slower Economic Growth: The United States in the 1970s*. Washington, D.C.: United States Government Printing Office, 1979.

Dickinson, G. M. *International Insurance Transactions and the Balance of Payments*. Geneva: Etudes et Dossiers n° 16, Association internationale pour l'étude de l'économie de l'assurance, June, 1978.

Economic Consulting Services, Inc. *The International Operations of U.S. Service Industries: Current Data Collection and Analysis*, Final Report. Washington, D.C., June, 1981.

Fuchs, Victor R. *The Service Economy*. New York: Columbia University Press, 1968.

Fuchs, Victor R., ed. *Production and Productivity in the Service Industries*. New York: National Bureau of Economic Research, 1969.

Galbraith, John Kenneth. "Thinking Ahead: The Way up from Reagan Economics." *Harvard Business Review: July-August 1982*.

Giarini, Orio. *Dialogue on Wealth and Welfare*. New York: Pergamon Press, 1980.

Ginzberg, Eli, and Vojta, George J. "The Service Sector of the U.S. Economy." *Scientific American*: March, 1981.

Goldschmidt-Clermont, Luisella. *Unpaid Work in the Household*. Geneva: Office international du travail, 1982.

Gray, H. P. "The Theory of International Trade Among Industrial Nations." *Weltwirtschaftliches Archiv*: Band 116/1980, Heft 3.

Greenfield, Harry T. *Manpower and the Growth of Producer Services*. New York, 1976.

Gustafsson, Bo, Ed. *Post-Industrial Society*. London: Croom Helm, 1979.

Hahn, Frank. "Reflections on the Invisible Hand." *Lloyd's Bank Review*: April 1982.

Hall, Margaret. "Are Goods and Services Different?", *Westminster Bank Review*: August, 1968.

Hill, A. T. P., and Mc Gibbon, J. M. "Growth of Sector Real Product, Measures and Methods in Selected OECD Countries." *Income and Wealth*: March, 1966.

Hirsch, Fred. *The Social Limits of Growth*. New York: Routledge and Kegan Park, 1977.

Kuznets, Simon. *Six Lectures on Economic Growth*. New York: The Free Press of Glencoe, Inc., 1960.

Lengellé, Maurice. *La Révolution Tertiaire*. Paris: Editions Génin, 1966.

—————. "The Development of the Service Sector in OECD Countries: Economic Implications." In *Western Economies in Transition: Structural Change and Adjustment Policies in Industrial Countries*, edited by Irvin Leveson and Jimmy W. Wheeler. Boulder, CO: Westview Press, 1980.

Leveson, Irving. *Productivity in Services, Issues for Analysis*. New York: Hudson Institute Papers, Hudson Institute, Inc., May, 1980.

Madec, Alain J. "Aspects économiques et juridiques des flux transfrontières de données." *Problèmes politiques et sociaux*, numéro 406. Paris: La Documentation française, 16 January, 1981.

Alfred Marshall, *Principles of Economics*. London: Macmillan, 1962. Philippe Lemoine.

McMahon, C. W., and Worswick, G. D. N. "The Growth of Services in the Economy." *District Bank Review*: December, 1960; March, 1961.

Marx, Karl. *Salaire, prix et profit*. Paris: Editions Sociales, 1952a.

—————. *Travail salarié et capital*. Paris: Editions Sociales, 1952b.

Mill, James Stuart. *Principles of Political Economy with Some of Their Applications to Social Philosophy*, vols. 1 and 2. Toronto: University of Toronto Press, Routledge and Kegan Paul, 1965.

—————. *Utiliarianism*. Glasgow: Fount Paperbacks, William Collins Sons & Co,

1962.

B. S. Minhas, *An International Comparison of Factor Costs and Factor Use.* Amsterdam: North-Holland Publishing Co., 1963.

Nusbaumer, Jacques. *L'Enjeu du Dialogue Nord-Sud, partage des richesses ou guerre économique.* Paris: Economica, 1981.

Organisation de coopération et de développement économiques (OCDE). *Problèmes de main-d'œuvre dans le secteur des services.* Paris, 1967.

Peccei, Aurelio. *100 pages pour l'avenir, Réflexions du Président du Club de Rome.* Paris: Economica, 1981.

Perroux, François. *Pour une philosophie du nouveau développement.* Paris: Aubier/ Les Presses de l'UNESCO, 1981.

Plant, Arnold. "The Economic Theory Concerning Patents for Inventions." *Economica*: February, 1934.

Prest, A R. "On charging for local government services." *The Three Banks Review*: March, 1982.

Rada, Juan. *Structure and Behavior of the Semiconductor Industry.* UNCTC/ Ballinger Press, May 1982.

Ruffié, Jacques. "Malthus est-il bien mort?" *Le Monde*: 17 July, 1982.

Sapir, André, and Lutz, Ernst. *Trade in Services: Economic Determinants and Development-Related Issues.* World Bank Staff Working Paper No. 480. Banque mondiale, August, 1981.

Shelp, Ronald Kent. *Beyond Industrialization.* New York: Praeger, 1981.

Shoup, Carl S. *Public Finance.* Chicago: Aldine Publishing Co., 1969.

Skerman, R. S. "The Development of a Common Market for Insurance within the EEC." *The Three Banks Review*: June, 1976.

Smith, Adam. *The Wealth of Nations.* Random House, New York: The Modern Library, 1960.

Smith, Anthony D. *The Measurement and Interpretation of Service Output Changes.* London: National Economic Development Office (NEDO), 1972.

Stigler, George J. *Trends in Employment in the Service Industries*, NBER Study No. 59. Princeton: General Series, Princeton University Press, 1956.

Tucker, K. A. *Traded Services in the World Economy.* Canberra Bureau of Industry Economics, Working Paper No. 16. 1979.

Wallerstein, I. *Capitalisme et économie-monde, 1450–1640.* Paris: Flammarion, 1980.

Wood, Charles T. "Relate Hospital Charges to Use of Services." *Harvard Business Review*: March–April, 1982.

Worswick, G. D. N., and Fane, C. G. "Goods and Services Once Again." *District Bank Review*: March, 1967.

Index